To Peter Leavy —
with the since...
all of us for your ...
at the Symposium.

Jacques
Doris Nagel
Larry
Ted

SPLIT MINDS/SPLIT BRAINS

SPLIT MINDS/SPLIT BRAINS
Historical and Current Perspectives

Edited by Jacques M. Quen, M.D.

NEW YORK UNIVERSITY PRESS
New York and London

Library of Congress Cataloging-in-Publication Data

Split minds/split brains.

Based on a symposium held Oct. 14–15, 1984 in Bear
Mountain, N.Y. on the twenty-fifth anniversary of the
Section on the History of Psychiatry of the New York
Hospital-Cornell Medical Center.
   Includes bibliographies and index.
   1. Dissociation Psychology—History—Congresses.
2. Multiple personality—History—Congresses. I. Quen,
Jacques M., 1928–   II. New York Hospital-Cornell
Medical Center. Section on the History of Psychiatry.
[DNLM: 1. Dissociative Disorders—history—congresses.
WM 11.1 S761 1984]
RC553.D5S65 1986   616.85′23   86-12532
ISBN 0-8147-6951-9

Book design by Ken Venezio

To Oskar Diethelm
psychiatrist, teacher, and historian

Contents

Acknowledgments

The Symposium Committee, responsible for planning and arranging the program (topics, speakers, room and lodging arrangements) as well as various other details, was composed of Doris Nagel-Baker, Lawrence Friedman, and Jacques M. Quen (Chair). Thanks are due to Peter Leavy for volunteering effective assistance during those last minute administrative crises.

Eric T. Carlson, Director of the Section for the past 25 plus years was a valued consultant to the Committee. Marilyn Kerr, our Section Secretary for more than 10 years, was once again a truly vital link, serving as a central information source for all of us, as well as managing mailings and photocopying, and providing cheerful interest and helpful suggestions.

Contributors

John C. Burnham, Ph.D., is Professor of History and Lecturer in Psychiatry at Ohio State University. He is the author of *Psychoanalysis and American Medicine, 1894–1918: Medicine, Science and Culture* (New York: International Universities Press, 1967) and *Jelliffe: American Psychiatrist and Physician* (Chicago: University of Chicago Press, 1983) with *His Correspondence with Jung and Freud* edited by William McGuire.

Eric T. Carlson, M.D., is Director of the Section on the History of Psychiatry and Clinical Professor of Psychiatry at the New York Hospital—Cornell Medical College. He is the Senior Editor of the annotated edition of *Benjamin Rush's Lectures on the Mind* (Philadelphia: American Philosophical Society, 1981), and the author of *Eighteenth-Century Psychiatric Pathogenesis: Benjamin Rush and His Predecessors*.

Adam Crabtree is in the private practice of group and individual psychotherapy in Toronto and is the author of *Multiple Man: The Enigma of Possession and Multiple Personality.* (Don Mills, Ontario: William Collins, 1984) and *Animal Magnetism, Early Hypnosis and Psychical Research From 1766–1925: An Annotated Bibliography.* (Millwood, N.Y.: Kraus International, 1985).

Hannah S. Decker, Ph.D., was a predoctoral Fellow of the Section on the History of Psychiatry and is now Associate Professor and Director of Graduate Studies in the Department of History of the University of Houston-University Park, Texas. She is an Adjunct Associate Professor in the Department of Psychiatry, Baylor College of Medicine. Dr. Decker is the author of *Freud in Germany: Revolution and Reaction in Science, 1893–1907.* (New York: International Universities Press, 1977) and the soon to be released *Psychoanalysis and Hysteria in Fin-de-Siècle Vienna: The Case of Dora.* (New York: The Free Press, 1985).

Lawrence C. Kolb, M.D., is a past Professor and Chairman of the Department of Psychiatry, Columbia University and a past Commissioner of Mental Hygiene of New York State. He is Distinguished Physician in Psychiatry at the VA Medical Center in Albany, N.Y.

Frank W. Putnam, M.D., is a staff psychiatrist in the Adult Psychiatry Branch of the National Institute of Mental Health at St. Elizabeths Hospital in Washington, D.C. He is the author of numerous papers on the psychophysiology of multiple personality disorder and is a cofounder of The National Foundation for the Prevention and Treatment of Multiple Personality.

Jacques M. Quen, M.D., is in the private practice of psychoanalysis and psychiatry. He is Associate Director of the Section on the History of Psychiatry and is Clinical Professor of Psychiatry at the New York Hospital—Cornell Medical Center. He coedited *American Psychoanalysis: Origins and Development* with Eric T. Carlson.

John J. Sidtis, Ph.D., is Assistant Professor of Psychology in the Department of Neurology, Division of Cognitive Sciences at the New York Hospital—Cornell Medical Center. He has published numerous papers on brain organization, localization, function, and physiology.

George Stade, Ph.D., is Professor of English Literature and Vice Chairman of the Department of English at Columbia University. He is the author of the novel, *Confessions of a Lady-Killer.* (New York: W. W. Norton, 1979) as well as numerous essays and reviews in literary criticism.

The Section on the History of Psychiatry, New York Hospital— Cornell Medical Center

The Section on the History of Psychiatry was founded on 1 July 1958. The present collection of papers grew out of a wish to mark the twenty-fifth anniversary of the Section on the History of Psychiatry. The Symposium was held on October 14–15, 1984, at the Bear Mountain Inn in Bear Mountain, N.Y.

The need for a Section on the History of Psychiatry devoted to the collection, cataloging, study, clarifying, and teaching the history of psychiatry was recognized by Dr. Oskar Diethelm, then Professor and Chairman of the Department of Psychiatry, New York Hospital— Cornell Medical Center. The Section was established on the same date as the beginning of the grant awarded to Eric T. Carlson to study the history of American psychiatry.

It was also at this time that our first predoctoral fellow, Norman Dain, joined the Section. His presence and experiences laid the groundwork for the conceptualization and later realization of our interuniversity pre- and postdoctoral training programs. The Section has offered medical student courses on the history of medical ideas as well as five to ten week electives for individual research in the history of psychiatry. This program has attracted students from other medical schools across the country. Many courses have been offered to psychiatric residents including the history of the concept and treatment of schizophrenia, the history of ideas in psychotherapy, and one on law and ethics in psychiatry.

Perhaps our best known activity has been our biweekly "working seminars" for research in progress. Because the material presented is work in progress, the discussions center on helpful suggestions for improving the project as well as other resources and relevant research studies from other disciplines. These spirited seminars are generally of substantial help to audience and speakers alike.

The Section has also sponsored symposia and lecture series on the mind-body problem; the origins and development of American psychoanalysis; Lacan and psychiatry; and the symposium on which this book is based.

Introduction

Jacques M. Quen, M.D.

The Section on the History of Psychiatry of the New York Hospital—Cornell Medical Center was founded on the belief that, in psychiatry, as in the rest of medicine, one can enhance appreciation of contemporary experiences by viewing them in the light of past understandings. There has been a recent mushrooming of interest in multiple personality and a cyclical medical interest in hypnosis. This symposium was designed to integrate the history of psychiatric/psychologic understanding of these phenomena with current conceptions.

Derived from association psychology, the term dissociation designates psychological phenomena long known but little understood in the history of medicine, which include multiple personality, hypnosis, fugue states, somnambulism, amnesia, altered states of consciousness, unconscious mentation, repression, and, more recently, posttraumatic stress disorders and "flashbacks." A favored situation in creative writing, cinema, and journalism is the apparent separation of discrete, integrated mental processes from other aspects of an individual's "normal" mental functioning, in which it appears that the individuals involved are unaware of important aspects of their own "conscious" behavior.

Eric T. Carlson, in the opening chapter, considers the history of dissociative phenomena up to 1880. Beginning with the magic of shamanism and the puzzle of epilepsy, he presents a fascinating narrative of the gradual evolution of concepts of dissociative behavior to the end of the nineteenth century. He surveys the contributions and relevant material from Aristotle through Hobbes, Hartley, Mesmer, Erasmus Darwin, Benjamin Rush, Galton, Kraepelin, Breuer, and Freud.

In her contribution, Hannah S. Decker suggests that interest in psychological dissociation was a reaction to the overvaluation of materialistic positivist science. She also provides a careful and substantial review of European literature dealing with dissociative phenomena as evidence of this new interest. She focuses largely on spiritism, hypnotism, and the career of Pierre Janet. She speculates about the failure of dissociation to maintain itself as a major scientific concern in the first half of the twentieth century. Decker finds within the medical scientific discussion of dissociation the essence of the mind—body controversy that has plagued human sciences since before the days of Descartes. She suggests that scientists were uncomfortable with their inability to quantify subjective data. Even Janet was unable to consider that a patient's reports might be valid and reliable scientific data.

Decker strolls through the nineteenth-century European cultural world comfortably and authoritatively, selecting from literature here, philosophy there, science here, and weaving these disparate fibers into a provocative question which, in a sense, she asks the reader to answer, or at least, to think about. I have the heartening sense that this is the first step in an investigation that she will be continuing and that she, herself, will be contributing to the answer.

John C. Burnham offers a somewhat different initial hypothesis for understanding the historical development of dissociation in the United States. He suggests that dissociation and its explanations can be understood best in the context of a general scientific enthusiasm for reductionism as an explanatory mode. As he says:

> Reductionism was a relentless pursuit of the idea that knowledge of components led to the knowledge of causes. . . . In the psychological-medical realm, the beginning concept was the soul, and the final intellectual product was dissociative phenomena.

Although it would appear at first (and second) blush that Burnham's proposition is diametrically opposed to that of Decker, he notes, early in his chapter, that,

> To such critics [of phrenology], it made little difference if materialism opened the way to division of the soul or if fragmentation of organs led to materialism.

So that he, too, finds that integral to the problem of dissociation is the tension between the forces tending toward an exclusively materialistic science and forces favoring a significant nonmaterial component.

Burnham leads us on an intriguing tour through the evolution of *modes* of thinking and perceiving in early twentieth-century intellectual America. The contrast with Decker's work is fascinating, as is his demonstration of the phenomenon and mechanism he describes as "dynamic atomicity," which serves admirably as a "thought key" to allow us to see the persistence of these American modes of thought into the present. The sense of a dynamism between conflict and collaboration is so clearly laid out that it facilitates understanding how this view was incorporated into the enthusiastic American response to the general theory of psychology proposed by Sigmund Freud in that same period.

Burnham leaves us with the novel suggestion that the eager adoption of Gordon Allport's emphasis on the individual, or the self,

may have been a late model, secularized version of the early nineteenth-century soul, but clearly the dynamic elements in it were a world away from traditional faculties.

Adam Crabtree discusses the concepts of dissociation in the early part of the twentieth century in terms of three separate theoretical issues; first, physiological versus psychological (or material versus nonmaterial) explanations of dissociation; second, the nature of the second or subconscious self; and, third, the Freudian view of dissociation as contrasted with Janet's.

Crabtree is also concerned with the question of the appropriate goal of treatment for the individual with multiple personalities. He calls attention to the unquestioned assumption that one of those personalities had to prevail and the others had to be resubmerged. It is striking to me that even today preference is often given to the preservation or reinforcement of one particular "personality" rather than an integration. At times one gets the impression that this is another area in which Theodore Sarbin would find the "reification" of a concept, as if the alternate personalities were "whole" ones.

Frank W. Putnam also concerns himself, in part, with the question of treatment and specifically refers to the goal of fusion of personalities. Putnam's interest lies largely in the interplay of the psychical and the physical in the multiple personality disorders (MPD). Furthermore, in a refreshing way, he embodies the ideal of the researcher who is clearly biased by his interests, but who, simultaneously, is skeptical of those ideas that would most simplify his task.

His intellectual forebears include Prince and Peterson who tried to determine whether there were physical correlates to the multiple personalities. Critical of their lack of controls, Putnam nevertheless respects their experiments with galvanic skin response. He is also intrigued by the repetitive relationship between a history of childhood trauma and hypnotizability as well as the occurrence of EEG abnormalities among the MPD population at twice the rate of the population at large.

Physical correlates are given extended attention by John J. Sidtis, a neuropsychologist investigating split-brain phenomena and hemispheric functions. He presents current knowledge in this area as it relates to the question of dissociation. It would not have been unreasonable to assume that the severing of connections between the two hemispheres would lead to dissociative effects. But Sidtis challenges our intuitive assumptions by telling us how little such dissociative phenomena are involved in the functioning of those people who have had that surgery.

Having presented the complicated and ingenious techniques for studying the functional effects of commissurotomy, and the consequent findings, Sidtis concludes that dissociative phenomena "represent a process far more complicated than simple disconnection," and they are not significantly physically causally related. He tells us that an understanding of psychological dissociation cannot yet be found in disconnection studies. Surgical separation of the two hemispheres does not appear to provide a model for dissociative phenomena.

In fact, Sidtis says, the drive for integration of the personality is remarkably strong and efficient in the postoperative commissurotomy individual. As a psychiatrist and psychoanalyst, I find this an important and somewhat humbling reminder of the existence of a psychological drive for integrated or "healthy" mental functioning, something that we tend to lose sight of when, as clinicians, we focus on psychopathology and pathological conflicts.

George Stade's chapter presents another perspective on and perception of dissociative phenomena, that of a literary critic. The earlier chapters focus on what was and what is, as well as different efforts to understand. Professor Stade injects the reminder that there are other aspects of dissociative phenomena than the ones we have already emphasized. He focuses on our fascination with horror and the uncanny.

Stade offers the work of Edgar Allan Poe to illustrate the use of multiple personality concepts in creative literature before the well-known names in medicine and psychology appeared on the scene. His presentation forcibly brings us back, from the laboratory and from the study of isolated phenomena to human experience with its broad range of emotions and intensities. He reminds us that multiple personality is not only a laboratory phenomenon but an experience that has a profound effect on the individual involved and those who are intimate witnesses. At the symposium, it was a gripping finale to a day of intensive thought and discussion.

The next morning we assembled for a panel discussion of the speakers and for extended audience participation. The discussion was energetic and provocative. Recognition is particularly due to William Frosch, Vice-Chairman of our Department of Psychiatry, who skillfully summarized the presentations, wove them into an integrated whole, and led the panel discussion with an éclat that added wit and learning in generous measure. Lawrence C. Kolb, related the relevance of the symposium to his own ongoing studies of Vietnam veterans and their posttraumatic stress disorders. His description of his clinical research experiences added another important dimension to what had been presented and we are grateful to him for allowing us to include his remarks here.

The symposium had all the earmarks of a successful meeting of scholars: all agreeing that despite the liberal time scheduled for discussion, still more would have been welcome and fruitful.

1. The History of Dissociation Until 1880

Eric T. Carlson, M.D.

Introduction

A standard popular dictionary defines dissociation as "the splitting off of certain mental processes from the main body of consciousness, with varying degrees of autonomy resulting."[1]

Of the various phenomena of dissociation, both small and large, normal and abnormal, the most spectacular are those associated with cases of multiple personality. One of the earliest, and often incorrectly cited as the first, was the case of Mary Reynolds, (1785–1854), a single woman of nearly twenty-six who had emigrated with her family from England and settled in the hills of Western Pennsylvania when she was thirteen. In the spring of 1811, she suffered a series of minor fits. After one severe attack she returned to consciousness both deaf and blind, conditions that lasted for nearly six weeks. A few weeks later, she awoke from a long sleep in a bewildered state, her behavior quite childlike and babbling like an infant. Most impressive was her loss of memory. She did not recognize her family, and could not speak or understand English. Five weeks later, she awoke one morning returned to her normal self with no recollection of the preceding events. A pattern became established in which her personality repetitively shifted and she spent increasing amounts of time in her second self. The new "person" learned English very quickly and exhibited many personality traits not evidenced before. No longer melancholic, the new Mary was cheerful, energetic, impish (she played practical jokes on people), and wrote poetry. She enjoyed the company of people, avoided solitude, was emotionally responsive and quick to show anger. After eighteen years of alternating personalities, she shifted permanently into her second state, although more subdued and mature at this point. She remained single, taught school for a time, and then devoted herself to the care of her nephew.[2]

What then is dissociation? This challenging, fascinating, and compelling topic encompasses many questions crucial to the understanding of the human condition. In this chapter, I will not try to narrow the definition but to broaden it. I say this not completely seriously, but I do not want to start with our mind set in too limited a fashion, but to open our thinking to the many elements that may be involved in varying degrees.

Let us pause, however, to list some of the issues involved, even though they be very broad. They may be divided into five areas:

1. The possible existence of parallel processing in brain activity both for incoming and outgoing physiological actions. These functions may be separated or split from one another, and include such modalities as motor, sensory, emotional, and intellectual.
2. These parallel processes may produce various behaviors ranging from those that appear to be totally under voluntary control to those that appear completely automatic. Learning and practice may shift an action from the former to the latter. For example, one has to learn to chew gum, but once the habit has been established, it can become quite automatic once the gum is inserted into the mouth and then operates largely outside the scope of awareness.
3. Awareness brings us into the complicated issues of what is in control, the role of attention and the degrees of awareness involved. We may seem totally aware, partially unaware, or even appear to be totally unaware. Here we approach the perplexing problems of consciousness and subconsciousness of the processes that go on and affect our behavior. As the processes become more complex and coalesce in different loci, consciousness itself may appear to be split so that two centers of knowledge seem to exist. How this knowledge acts and how it may be recalled raise questions about memory and the existence of amnesia or unawareness between these two loci.
4. Questions of personal identity or self-concept arise when these two or more loci expand and seem to take on personlike roles of their own.
5. This deals finally more with the quantitative degrees of human functions. We see patterns where functions are either diminished (even to the point of being abolished), or enhanced to a degree where they may appear superhuman and therefore supernatural.

Many variations on these issues will appear in this chapter and those that follow.

I will present a selective overview of the topic up until 1880. My discussion will be subdivided into a brief historical review of some of the phenomena observed and then a longer but still limited look at explanations of association and dissociation that were advanced during the first eight decades of the nineteenth century.

The Dissociative Phenomena

As indicated by the outline given in table 1.1 the wide range of pre-1880 phenomena that today might be designated as involving dissociation includes areas that have heretofore been considered religious, medical, or simply aspects of daily life. For example, shamanism is one of the oldest human rituals, and, in one form or another, seems to appear in a wide variety of preliterate tribes across the world even though the specific term is Siberian in origin. The shamans, as healers and priests, used dissociative techniques such as trances and spirit

Table 1.1 The Phenomena of Dissociation Recognized Today

A. Varieties of Religious Dissociation
1. shamanism
2. asceticism and the limits of individual identity
3. possession
4. revivalism and conversion
5. glossolalia or speaking in tongues
6. the spiritualistic medium
7. near death experiences
8. crystal gazing, imagery, visions, and hallucinations
B. The Secular and Medical Dissociations
1. spontaneous trances: ecstasy, catalepsy, and somnambulism
2. induced trances: animal magnetism
3. amnesias
4. fugue states
5. multiple personality
C. The Dissociations of Everyday Life
1. dreams and other sleep association phenomena
2. reverie
3. absentmindedness and inattention
4. habitual actions
5. automatisms, the planchette, and the ouija board

communication to aid them in their daily roles. Although shamanism was meant to cure many disorders which would be considered of medical origin today, the explanations then proposed were largely "spiritual" and magical as were the techniques used in treatment. The philosophical setting was holistic and religious. The potential shamans were chosen for their future role both by hereditary factors and spirit selection. If a child had a known shaman ancestor, or had epilepsy which suggested the presence of a shaman forebear, then the chances of selection were heightened. The chosen child was also likely to be sickly, withdrawn, and contemplative before actual spirit selection occurred, which took place near puberty. The initiation period was accompanied by seizures, disturbances of sleep (sleeptalking, sleepwalking, prolonged sleep), amazing dreams, trance states, and a wide variety of physical complaints. The shaman-to-be was then trained to use his skills through "epileptoid trances" during which he learned to travel through, and deal with, the spirit world. Early training by contemporary shamans taught him all the lore and ritualistic techniques of the profession. Manipulating and negotiating with the spirit world was the major role of the shaman. Spirits could speak through the shaman's voice, or enable him to speak in foreign tongues and in animal voices. Symbolically, the shaman dealt with death and resurrection and traveled to the upper and lower worlds of the spirits. His experiences included visions, revelations, divinations, and clairvoyance, all used to assist in dealing with misfortune and illness.[3]

Similar dissociative phenomena to those noted in shamanism were reported in the witchcraft epidemics and in spontaneous and induced somnambulism in the Christian Western world. Witchcraft is of special interest because possession by the devil, or by his or her assistant spirits, creates a form of religious multiple personality which can easily be classified as dissociative. Belief in witchcraft was not considered a heresy until the thirteenth century when the Roman Christian Church reversed its previous policy and made bewitching a heretical act. Bewitchment was a state caused by a witch or wizard who had made an alliance with the power of darkness (the devil) to create mischief, illness, and death. The Church needed a guide to deal with the identification and treatment of possession and produced *Rituale Romanum* in 1614, a book which brought together knowledge spanning nearly 1,500 years.[4] Shortly thereafter, a theologian, Maximilian von Eynatten, wrote a book that included many of the same phenomena listed in the *Romanum*. In it he extended the list of criteria for possession. We cannot reproduce them all, but they included the following major divisions:

1. Deep sleep, violence, and animal behavior.
2. Restlessness, spells of immobility and/or rigidity, excessive powers, tormentations (including suicidal attempts) and howling like a beast.
3. Excessive nonstop talking, glossolalia or speaking in tongues, sudden expanded intelligence and a knowledge of supposedly secret information (the *Rituale Romanum* included clairvoyance), or, extreme distress and torment when placed in religious settings. (Category 3 provided the most important evidence for being bewitched.)

In contrast, the shaman was not thought to be possessed by his helping spirits as in witchcraft, but rather to summon the spirits, somewhat like a nineteenth-century medium. For that matter, according to Mirea Eliade, the shaman himself seems to take possession of the spirit. In the process, he often seems to have an "alter ego" which can be either humanlike or bestial in form.

In the same way, many dissociative similarities can be found in the two somnambulisms, both spontaneous and induced. Spontaneous somnambulisms were often associated with sleep disturbances and prolonged sleep, as well as spastic and convulsive behavior. The subject might be unresponsive to usual stimuli, but at the same time rapidly experience enhanced abilities even to the point that these abilities appeared miraculous. On the American scene in the early nineteenth century, duplicating much that was already reported in France, there were somnambulists such as Rachel Baker, who preached in her sleep in a manner that transcended her background and education.[5] Even more spectacular were the accomplishments of Nancy Hazard who was able to transpose her senses so that she could "see" colors through her fingertips,[6] while Jane C. Rider found her way around in the dark and was able to read in total darkness.[7] The mediums, after mid-century, impressed many with their ability to contact the spirit world, enabling the spirits to verbalize through them.

Induced or artificial somnambulism became a great fad after the exhibitions by Franz Anton Mesmer in Paris in the early 1780s, demonstrating the effects of what he called animal magnetism, renamed hypnotism by James Braid in 1843. Enthusiasm for hypnotism came in cyclical waves. During the earliest enthusiastic period in the 1780s, magnetizers recognized certain patterns in the mesmeric experience. Not until a later period in the 1810s and 1820s was an explicit attempt made to characterize the phenomena of hypnotism. The person who was most successful in doing this was Alexandre Bertrand, who wrote two important books on the subject in which he approached the topic with a concern for the use of scientific evidence, as then conceived.[8] Bertrand concluded that there were twelve different consistent phenomena associated with hypnotism. He did not include the convulsive movements seen so often in the mesmeric crisis of a generation before. But spasmodic movements were still common in the case accounts of his era and continued to be throughout the century. Bertrand included three clear supernatural findings (prevision, eyeless vision and telepathy), plus an ability to prescribe appropriate medication which also seemed quite magical.

From this brief survey there clearly emerges a pattern of biological and psychological behavior that underlies a variety of phenomena, ranging from the magical, mystical and religious considerations through trance states to differing degrees of inattention. Science focused intermittently on these states of altered consciousness, but was repeatedly defeated because either they seemed too close to magic or were tainted by clear imposture.

Mesmerism arrived on the scene late in the Enlightenment of the eighteenth century, at a time when there was a growing emphasis on describing man and his behavior from a naturalistic point of view. The philosophers and physicians were studying the mind, and many (especially the Scottish philosophers) wrote about forms of a faculty psychology which led toward a more discrete analysis of psychological functioning. At the turn of the century, Pierre-Jean-Georges Cabanis, French physician-philosopher, proclaimed that the brain was the organ of the mind. At the same time, Franz Joseph Gall was developing his system of phrenology which attempted to locate individual mental faculties in specific portions of the brain. During this time, a growing reaction against the intellectualism of the Enlightenment led to greater attention to mysterious and religious themes. This fascination with mystical and horrific phenomena was most vividly portrayed in popular novels of the Romantic period. Yet the interest in somnambulism, both natural and artificial, was part of two contradictory movements, as investigators tried to prove that the supernatural world existed.

In this setting, a condition was first described that would have a major impact on nineteenth-century thought and scientific investigation—the earliest description of multiple personality. Undoubtedly earlier cases will emerge and one must also recognize that there are parallel cases in bewitchment where two devils were reported to possess and speak through one person.[9] The existence of two minds within one person, or double consciousness as it was first called, came to light with two cases reported in 1791, one in Germany and one in the United States reported in Springfield, Massachusetts.[10] As more cases were discovered, interest in hypnosis grew, especially the creation of similar states, as well as the study of memory and amnesia, personal identity and diverse mental disconnections. We cannot consider all the phenomena that are important to the development of the concept of dissociation; similarly we exclude most of the various explanations advanced to explain these conditions. (Most of the ones then advanced are listed in table 1.2.) Only the themes of association and dissociation will be discussed, and even here attention will be directed largely to the Anglo-American scene. Various factors involved in the separation or

Table 1.2 Nineteenth-Century Explanations of Dissociative Phenomena

A. A Faked Experience
B. Appeal to Religion
C. Medical Models
    1. sleep and dreams, somnambulism
    2. paroxysms and intermittent insanity
    3. hysteria
    4. drug induced
    5. phrenology, the diseased brain and the dual brain
    6. animal magnetism and the induced trance state
D. Philosophical and Psychological Considerations
    1. attention and awareness, consciousness, and the subconscious
    2. the development of the self, personal identity
    3. memory and amnesia
    4. association and disassociation
    5. the crowd, imitation, imagination, and suggestion

splitting of associations are explored as well as how aggregates can continue to exist and have a life of their own, particularly out of conscious awareness. We end our account by returning to the broader picture, particularly in France as we approach our terminal date of 1880 when concentration on this subject experienced a major acceleration.

Explanation: Association and Dissociation of Ideas

Of all the nineteenth century explanatory models listed in table 1.2, only the precursors of dissociation will be discussed in any depth. Once one begins to examine the historical background of association and dissociation, one discovers a considerable morass. Let us start by looking briefly at the history of the concept of association of ideas so that we can understand better how clumps of ideas could be separated and have a life of their own. For many centuries thoughtful writers have puzzled over how language developed and ideas emerged, and how we as individuals made connections between thoughts, through systems of memory and then learned from the process. Aristotle, in his struggles to understand memory, stressed the distinction between remembering and recalling.

Recalling is the more active process demanding a search for related ideas, a process which Aristotle called deliberation and which he felt was limited only to man in the animal kingdom. There was order involved in these processes, and therefore laws. He found three that played a role in recalling associations: contiguity, similarity, and contrast. In addition, he recognized that recollection was more assured if the original stimulus had been repeated, if the sequence of stimuli were in a fixed order, and, finally, if there was a strong emotional connection. But it was the British school of philosophers and empiricists who contributed most to the growth of emphasis on associationism. First Thomas Hobbes, in his seventeenth century political and materialistic psychology, concluded that mental activities were the products of motions in the central nervous system. He then proposed that it was only the experiences gained from the action of the senses that built the simple, and gradually the complex, ideas in the mind. He spoke of "trains of thought," which would subsequently be called associations. Fifty years later, in 1700, John Locke coined the expression "the association of ideas" when he used it as a title for a chapter that he added to the fourth edition of *An Essay Concerning Human Understanding.*

Even greater were the contribution and impact of the writings of David Hume. Hume sought to apply laws to the operation of the human mind, as Newton had done with the heavenly bodies, and believed he had found the solution with his law of association of ideas, which represented a basic aspect to the human experience. Like his immediate predecessors, Hume believed in the primacy of a sensory impression on which associations were built through three basic laws— similarity, contiguity in time and place, and causality. He advanced the eighteenth-century concern with habit by stressing its importance as the principle that connected ideas. The physician-philosopher David Hartley, while still maintaining a strong religious position, extended the emphasis on the body even further in his *Observation of Man* written in 1749. In essence he made association possible through connecting vibrations in the nervous system, and helped pave the way for both reflex theories and those of stimulus and response later in the century. Vibrations first made possible the sensory impressions and the then continuing reverberations created memory and recollection. Robert Watson credits Hume with establishing a system of psychology based on associationism.[11]

In the nineteenth century, both James Mill and his son, John Stuart Mill, along with Alexander Bain, helped keep the Hartleyian tradition alive. But association theory was changing as many writers realized its limitations in explaining all the ramifications of learning and remembering. Soon a resurgence of interest in conditioning would provide competitive hypotheses to explain learning. At the same time, the issue of association remained active in diverse areas: in Francis Galton's experiments on word association begun in 1879 which eventually led to the entire growth of psychological testing, in the study of reaction time by Theodore Ziehen, in the various association studies of Aschaffenberg and Kraepelin, followed by those of Carl Jung, and eventually in the researches of the galvanic skin response around 1910.

Disunion of Thoughts. Most of the writers discussed dealt with the ways in which ideas came together, stayed together, and could be recaptured. At the same time, growing attention was paid to how the connections could be disrupted or come apart. The history of this trend remains to be written, but some landmarks can be identified. Late in the Enlightenment, the distinguished physician, Erasmus Darwin, grandfather of Charles, writing in 1794, spoke of "associate tribes and trains of motions." Motion and association were cornerstones of an elaborate hypothesis he was trying to develop that he thought would be meaningful to most, if not all, medical conditions. He also applied these cornerstones to the world of ideas and behavior. Although he did not give a name to it, he struggled with understanding how similar processes could be simultaneous but separate. Actually, he spoke of two kinds of association, synchronous and successive, but he did not name the process of separation, only saying that associations besides combining under certain laws, could also be broken. Darwin also spoke of trains being "disunited," reminiscent of the thinking of Hobbes, yet he took many of his ideas from Hume. Many of his examples showed his awareness that attentional processes in everyday life could work in two directions—through enhancement and interference. If one wants to enhance the possibility of hearing a faint and distant noise, Darwin recommended that one should "suppress other trains of ideas." For example, holding one's breath to increase the acuity of concentration. Yet, concentration also tends to shut out awareness of parallel activity. Darwin gave two examples which illustrated the increasing separation. The first was the common experience of attending to something when a fly lands on your forehead and you brush it away "without breaking" the train of ideas. The other has to do with an intensely preoccupied student who does not hear the noise of a distant artillery barrage.

For Darwin, these kinds of experiences were similar to having a dream at night and not being able to remember it the next day. The separation from consciousness is not irrevocable, however, for "some analogous idea may introduce afresh this forgotten train" from the dream. Reveries also are allied to dreams in that neither are accompanied by a proper and adequate sense of time; the experience is timeless. Daytime reveries can be almost totally absorbing, but if sufficiently boring, they appear related to sleep as then we may doze off into a nap. If intensively preoccupied, we may overlook the need to eat or may stay up beyond our normal bedtime hour. The dreams of sleep are different from reverie in that we lose our normal waking ability to compare our imaginary thought, not being able to "voluntarily recollect our waking ideas at all." Darwin's implications are that our dream

world is separate from our conscious waking world; dreams are different from reveries in that our visual abilities are strikingly enhanced
in our dreams. Darwin was probably right in assuming that our dreams
are primarily visual, and that they are discontinuous with our waking
world, although sometimes we know that we can be aware while
dreaming, because we know we are dreaming. We are equally certain
that our waking self can have a difficult time making contact with the
contents of our dreams.[12]

We may consider our waking daydreams and self-absorptions as a
form of reverie, as did Erasmus Darwin, but generally he used the term
to mean more intense conditions. His definition was "that reverie is an
effort of the mind to relieve some painful sensation, and is hence allied
to convulsion, and to insanity." Also he claimed "that reverie is a
disease of the epileptic or cataleptic kind." This proposal was based, it
would appear, on one case which he reported in some detail: that of a
seventeen-year-old woman, whose attacks started with several convulsions which were followed by a cataleptic period. Reveries next ensued
in which she would have emotional discussions with imaginary people
or quote endless pages from English poetry. She was unresponsive to
severe painful stimuli during the attack, and when she recovered,
usually following a series of repeated convulsions, she had complete
amnesia for her preceding period. Although this appeared to be a form
of somnambulism, Darwin rejected it as being a sleep state because the
faculty of volition continued to be present. These attacks continued on
alternate days when she would pick up her conversation where she had
left off on the occasion of her previous attack. Darwin commented: "She
appeared to her friends to possess two minds." Darwin unfortunately
abandoned these deliberations at this point, but with these tantalizing
words:

The associated trains of our ideas may have sympathies, and their primary and
secondary parts affect each other in some manner—and may thus disturb the
deductions of our reasonings, as well as the streams of our imaginations; present
us with false degrees of fear, attach unfounded value to trivial circumstances;
give occasion to our early prejudices and antipathies; and thus embarrass the
happiness of our lives. A copious and curious harvest might be reaped from this
province of science, in which, however, I shall not at present wield my sickle.

It would be nearly a century before this harvest would begin in earnest,
even though many contributed to various limited attempts in the
meantime.[13]

An early attempt was made by Thomas Beddoes, an admirer of Darwin who copied his style yet criticized the details of Darwin's writings. Beddoes, in a series of essays published in 1802–1803, contributed scattered but meaningful comments on the subject. Two features of his work stand out. First, he believed that emotions play a significant role in strengthening associations. "For feelings that have accompanied ideas at different times, have prodigious power in bringing these ideas together." "The associating power of the feelings—is the most neglected, and perhaps at the same time the most pregnant topic in the doctrine of the mind." Beddoes also predicted that a study of emotions would be the "chief secret for unriddling the inconsistencies of dreams." Secondly, he mentioned the variations that could occur in associations. They might be so strong as to have "such attachment to one object" that everything else about the subject is forgotten. This fits with Darwin's milder reverie, or everyday daydreams. On the other hand, the associations could be weakened as seen in imbecility, or idiotism, or in "long continued nervous disorders" and were more likely if frequent, or severe, or in childhood. Even further, there would be a "disunion of trains" which Beddoes believed came about from some cause acting behind the product. He does not attempt to take this further, however. There could also be "destruction of the associating quality" which could be so severe in mania that the afflicted cannot even finish a sentence.[14]

Benjamin Rush also paid attention to these matters, citing Hobbes, but following his mentor David Hartley. Rush classified association as "something" in the brain that sympathizes with other parts of the body. He concluded "we are mere thinking machines" who are "unable to stop the current of our thoughts." But this "involuntary nature" had established laws which were related to those of motion. For Rush, the association of ideas was like that of sympathy which is the "association of motions in the human body." He stated that ideas and bodily motions had five characteristics in common, which sound very much like Hume's list. He then proceeded to review sixteen different influences on association which included pain and pleasure, signs, interest, and habit. These were from his lectures on what we today would call physiological psychology.[15] In his psychiatric text of 1812, he devoted a chapter to what he named "Dissociation," which may be the earliest medical use of the term.[16] Rush used it for patients that Americans called "flighty," "hairbrained," or a "little cracked." It came from "an association of unrelated perceptions, or ideas, from the inability of the mind to perform the operations of judgment and reason." It was seen in patients with "great volubility of speech" and rapid bodily movements. Rush (who had assisted Jean-Pierre Blanchard, and arranged for medical studies of the experience, when Blanchard made the first American balloon ascension in Philadelphia in January 1792), went on to say "the mind in this disease may be considered as floating in a balloon, and at the mercy of every object and thought that acts upon it." He continued by observing that the reaction occurred often in paroxysms and would frequently be followed by a period of "low spirits." Rush admitted that this seemed to be the same condition that was called "démence" by Philippe Pinel. We can see it as representing the type of disorder seen in a manic attack or schizophrenic excitement, in which the association of ideas does indeed become disturbed and fragmented.

This was Rush's major statement on dissociation, but scattered in other places one finds further evidence of his interest in the subject as it relates to the separation and fragmentation of larger ideational components which are accompanied by the power or energy to act. Rush reported two conditions, one related to shifts in the language spoken in fevers and other serious illnesses and the other to the phenomena of somnambulism. One of the most striking examples of language shift came from the case of Dr. Jean Baptiste Scandella, an Italian who visited Rush in Philadelphia in July 1798, and went on to New York during the yellow fever epidemic in the fall and died from this disease. Rush reported that Scandella spoke only English in the early stages of his illness, French in the middle portion and then Italian during the last day of his life.[17]

Rush also discussed phenomena where the disconnections were even greater. In one of these experiences, he had been consulted by the daughter of an English military officer who had "been educated in the habits of gay life" but who married a Methodist minister and zealously devoted herself to their ceremonies and principles. She had, however, "paroxysms of madness" in which she ridiculed the Methodists, resumed the aspects of a sprightly and social life, of which no details are given by Rush except that she reverted to speaking French. When she returned to her original state, she became as demure and religious as ever and had absolutely no memory for the period of her attack.[18]

Rush had also learned of the case of a young man in Springfield, Massachusetts, who, in 1791, had intermittent spells of different consciousness, each continuous unto itself in memory, but each state unaware of the other. The Reverend Joseph Lathrop who reported the case thought "he seemed to have *two distinct minds* which acted by turns independently of each other." Rush combined the observations on somnambulism, the case of this young man, and other cases where foreign languages emerged as if from nowhere and concluded that these "appear indeed as if they depended upon *two* minds; but they may be explained, by supposing they were derived from preternatural or excessive motions in different parts of the brain, inhabited by one and the same mind." In this one statement Rush reveals both his devotion to physiology and the growing emphasis on the nervous system, as well as the influence of a strong religious position which would make it hard to think in terms of the mind, or soul, as being divisible into two.[19]

Reflex Action in the Realm of Ideas. The growing interest in the biology of the nervous system and the study of reflex motor responses gradually contributed a reflex model for questions about the rapidity of thought and the force of ideas which could lead to automatic action and even outside consciousness. The observation of a simple muscular reflex which was undoubtedly known to ancient man, was brought more forcibly into science through the speculation of Descartes and with knowledge accelerating further in the late eighteenth century. What in essence happened was the combining of old ideas about the role of bodily sympathy, which had roots both in magic and physiology, with the functions of the nervous system.

Of more immediate interest to the medical profession was how the nervous system played a role in coordinating the sympathies both of the bodily functions and eventually including those of the brain and the mind. The body's capacity to respond to stimuli was clarified in the eighteenth century by Albrecht von Haller's proposal that there were two types; irritability, which brought a clearer response in muscular and allied tissue, and sensibility, which was the response provoked in the nervous system that led to sensation and thought. The Scottish physician, Robert Whytt, experimented on the topic, partly in an attempt to disprove Haller, and ended, for all practical purposes, in demonstrating the existence of the spinal reflex although he did not use modern terminology. Most of his attentions were addressed to the grosser movements in the body (and he actually spoke of a number of reflex functions), but he also pointed out the role of the passions and ideas in connecting with the motions of the body. He made hysteria and hypochondriasis, like his associate William Cullen, primarily diseases of motion and not thought. But clearly the brain mediated connections between ideas, emotions, and bodily motions. The connections could be consistent and enduring.[20]

It was this type of thinking that enabled Erasmus Darwin to accept, expand upon, and combine stimulus-response theory with that of associationism. He even spoke of a "reflex idea" some fifty years before Thomas Laycock introduced the concept.

Thomas Laycock took the traditional association of ideas and combined them with the growing enthusiasm for the reflex. As he stated in 1845: "Like the association of movements, the true explanation of the association of ideas is to be found in the doctrine of the reflex functions of the brain."[21]

Marshall Hall's writings on the spinal reflex in 1833 were basic to this development, but the growing attention to hypnotism in England after 1837 was also to play a key role. Laycock had been a student at the University Hospital in London in 1833–1835, and therefore had the distinguished but controversial John Elliotson as his teacher. He also knew about Elliotson's research with the two O'Key sisters in 1837, and decided he had to discover how much of this phenomenon was feigned and how much was due to cerebral action. In his reports of 1838–1839, Laycock compared "the involuntary but purposive behavior exhibited in hypnotic trances to the analogous behavior of hysterics." Those observations strengthened his belief that Hall was wrong to limit his excitomotor reflexes to the spinal cord and then to assume none could take place higher up in the nervous system. When Laycock proclaimed the existence of the reflex motions in the cerebrum, he used as one of his main arguments the phenomena that gave rabies its popular name of hydrophobia. Laycock not only recalled the traditional view that attempts to swallow water often led to painful gaspings and convulsive motions, but added that even the sight of water could precipitate the same responses. Perhaps these could be seen as similar to an excitomotor reflex with the withdrawal of a limb automatically when faced with pain from a hot object. The catch, however, was that the nerves of vision were in the head and therefore the brain was presumed to be involved in some more direct way. Laycock took the question to the ultimate step: some patients had the full range of their distressing reactions just to the suggestion of drinking a glass of water. Laycock did not say so at this juncture, but he must also have been thinking of how actions could be suggested to persons under hypnosis which they would then later carry out automatically without any apparent awareness or memory as to why. (This occurrence had been reported as early as 1787.)[22]

This manner of reasoning enabled Laycock to conclude that "the posterior gray matter or its analogue in the brain may then be considered as the seat of associations and train of ideas." It was here that "ideas may be inscribed, and require only sensory impressions to rouse *them*." Laycock called for researchers to turn their attention to what could be learned from the insane, the somnambulist, the dreamer, and persons in a delirium. Laycock suggested using a form of "cerebral analysis" based on a chemical model which he had proposed in an earlier form in 1840. "The reagent is the impression made on the brain; the molecular changes following the application of the reagent are made known to us as ideas." "In cerebral analysis we *feel* the change, or observe its results on the efferent nerves." In this process

the transition of structure and function is gradual and consequently, no strong line of demarcation can be drawn between the manifestation of its various functions. The automatic acts pass insensibly into the reflex, the reflex into the instinctive, the instinctive are *quasi* emotional, the emotional are intellectual. This gradation of structure and function observed in the nervous system, is observed also with reference to all other structures of his body.

Laycock divided the substrata of the nervous system into two types, those he called the kinetic and the ideogenic. "New substrata may be formed by the reaction of external stimuli on those already existing; or, in other words, new instincts may be acquired and be transmissible." Laycock also added that the substrata may continue both to act long after there was any such need, or in other cases, could lie dormant for extensive periods until called into action by the proper stimulus. Again, Laycock appeared to take hypothesis into the field of chemistry by proposing a "molecular organization." Learning, therefore, led to the formation of new substrata, both in humans and in many lower species.[23]

There followed an ongoing debate about the role of the reflex in the nervous system, about how high up it would function and whether it could still take place if it reached areas that subserved consciousness. The spinal reflex was thought to be totally automatic and therefore in the realm of unconsciousness. The British physician who played the most important role in terms of bringing the debate into medical and scientific awareness was Dr. William Carpenter who had also been cited by Laycock in his 1845 article. Carpenter eventually stressed the existence of three levels of reflex action in the nervous system. The first followed from Marshall Hall, and was equally accepted by Laycock, and was called the excitomotor reflex which was located in the spinal cord and perhaps the lower brain. The second, Carpenter named sensorimotor or consensual and occurred in the midbrain. He believed the second was all unconscious, but Laycock thought they could be either conscious or outside awareness. Carpenter did not initially put cerebral reactions into his hierarchy, but he changed his mind after 1851 in part because of the impact of studies on hypnotism. He was impressed that volition appeared suspended in the hypnotic state and that the subject became "a mere *thinking automaton*" whose flow of ideas resulted from external suggestions only. At this point, Carpenter added a third level, that for intelligence, presumably located in the cerebrum. Carpenter was slower in coming to this stance because he had accepted the experimental evidence from the French physiologist, Pierre Flourens, that the cerebrum could not be excited experimentally. Where Laycock speculated on the resulting actions to stimulation and used the term ideogenic, Carpenter instead spoke of ideomotor and thereby paralleled the previous nomenclature for the two lower levels. Carpenter admitted that the ideomotor response could be unconscious, thereby agreeing with Laycock. But they differed according to Roger Smith in that Laycock believed these three levels were continuous in their actions while Carpenter saw them as discontinuous. Carpenter also introduced the term "unconscious cerebration" for these cerebral reflex functions. It had quite a vogue when Carpenter revised his famous and influential physiology textbook into the fifth edition of 1855. In this massive tome, Carpenter devoted 140 pages to discussing the cerebrum and its relationships to the rest of the nervous system.[24]

Reversion, Dissolution, and Regression. Laycock continued through-out his life to make further comments on the cerebral reflex and maintained his divisions of ideogenic and kinetogenic. Following the pattern elucidated for the spinal cord, ideogenic activity in the brain was seen as following a sensory mode, while the latter was motor in nature. The sensory cerebral reflex led to a type of cerebral response which was the association of ideas. Herein ideas, along with their accompanying emotions, became the primary stimuli leading to a re-sponse. These ideas could be contemporary or could arise from the past, through memory.[25]

In addition to the concepts discussed above, Laycock proposed that there were two basic laws pertaining to the brain: evolution and rever-sion. Laycock believed that the body itself did not evolve during the course of a lifetime, but that the brain could and would in the sense that it continued to learn and to store this new knowledge by changing the molecular organization in the "substrata" of the brain. For Laycock, this was a form of evolution. Apparently under the influence of La-marckian concepts, which he discovered some time after 1845, he came to believe that current memories could be passed on to our offspring. When these memories became part of the ongoing species, then ac-cumulated ancestral memories could emerge, or, otherwise expressed, he accepted the concept of acquired characteristics.[26]

If the laying down of memories was a form of evolution Laycock also believed that a falling back on earlier memories that could still be recalled was a reversal of the process, and therefore to be named "reversion." Laycock later claimed that he had formulated the notion of "reversion" in his 1845 paper, but it is not as explicit as he probably remembered it in retrospect. It is true that he spoke of memory as existing in the "molecular organization" of the brain and that he spoke of the reflex gasp of the hydrophobic patient at the sight or idea of water.[27] By 1874 he ascribed this action to having its foundation in the amphibious phase of evolution wherein the species learned to shut out water automatically when submerged in order to survive. One may speculate that his early concepts were influenced further after 1859 by the writings of his fellow countrymen, Charles Darwin and Herbert Spencer, who wrote on reversion and dissolution as part of their evolutionary proposals. He certainly knew their works, and cited both of them. This is one pathway, as Stanley Jackson has aptly pointed out, that led to the development of Freud's formulation of regression.[28] In his writings of 1874 Laycock also stressed the relevance of reversion to the current writings on atavism.

In summary, Laycock postulated two kinds of memory: that from ancestral remnants and that from current life which was produced by sensory impressions plus attention creating a brain record. Laycock spoke of two kinds of recall; those from sensory processes and those from similar motor ones. By the latter he meant the immediate recollections induced by "external impression." The sensory form (which involved "change in the sensory vesicular neurine" in the brain) was more complex, as recall here was internal and the same as the "association of ideas." Extensive ideation could follow from this process.

Reversion, according to Laycock, could play a role in a number of conditions, both normal and abnormal. He cited sleep and the various phenomena accompanying dreams. To this he added the spontaneous somnambulisms. He also stressed that, when in heightened emotional states, normal people would be likely to demonstrate reversion. As might be expected, Laycock paid attention to the changes that occurred during the life span. He claimed that evolution ended in old age when recent memory faded and new learning declined, and the aged person lived increasingly in the memories of childhood. This Laycock found "analogous to ancestral reversion, or heredity proper."

More unusual, if not abnormal, were the changes in hypnotism and, for that matter, the results of imitation and suggestion which he believed involved cerebral reflexes. Laycock also extended his discussion of reversion to include the phenomena of idiotism, insanity, and criminal behavior. Believing that reversion explained atavism, he thereby entered into the topic of degeneration which would become so dominant in the psychiatry of the next three decades.

Laycock's postulated hypotheses of the cerebral reflex, and of evolution and reversion in the nervous system, contributed to the march toward dissociation. By bringing the reflex into "cerebral processes," he proposed a model that made fast and automatic responses possible in the realm of ideas. Automatic thinking, speaking, writing, and more complex actions became topics of increasing interest to psychologists later in the century. As early as 1868, Prosper Despine had been speaking of "psychological automatisms." Laycock proclaimed most of these responses as being unconscious, that ideas could be charged with varying amounts of energy, and that ideas could act as causes of human disturbances, both psychological and physiological.

The Last Decade: 1870–1880

It will be helpful in conclusion to present a brief overview of Continental medical thought leading into the final decade of 1870–1880.

German and French history of these years is better known, but there is much research to be done in order to understand the details of the background to the dissociation concept. Wilhelm Griesinger wrote on the psychical reflex in 1843, two years before Laycock's paper. Through his professorships at Zurich and Berlin, he went on to become the dominant psychiatrist on the Germanic scene, and eventually his influence spread far beyond national boundaries. According to Kenneth Levin, the second edition of Griesinger's famous textbook (published in German in 1861 and translated into English in 1867) was a complicated mixture of reflex psychology and the psychology of J. F. Herbart.[29] Herbart wrote his main works on psychology before 1835, but they continued to have an impact throughout the century and especially through pedological teachings. Ellenberger describes his associationist psychology as "energetic-dynamic." Herbart proposed that mental representations in the mind jostle with each other for the right to reach consciousness, those with greater energy emerging victorious. The suggestion of energetic ideas originating was a normal process and was not thought to be pathogenic at first. This was part of the speculative pathway that ideas had energy behind them and normally would not be pathogenic. The latter concept would be developed later by Moritz Benedikt who wrote on the importance of the pathogenic secret and the role of fantasies in hysteria. Benedikt also became a good friend of Jean-Martin Charcot. The German stage for this final decade was set in 1869 by the appearance of a most popular volume, *The Philosophy of the Unconscious,* written by Eduard van Hartmann.

In France, Eugène Azam, a surgeon from Bordeaux, became interested in the use of hypnotism for inhibiting pain during surgery. Azam had a patient referred to him in 1858 named Félida who evidenced multiple personality. He followed her case intermittently for 35 years, and, in 1887, published a book about her with an introduction by Charcot.[30] In 1876, he had reported and discussed her case in four

articles in which he used various terminology such as double consciousness (which goes back as far as the case of Mary Reynolds in 1816),
periodic amnesia, doubling of life, and the splitting of the personality
into two. Obviously, we are moving much closer to a specific formulation of dissociation. The movement was further abetted by the fad for
spiritualism which reached France in the mid-1850s. The phenomena
of spiritism, whether it be spirits of the dead speaking through mediums, or spirit-rapping or table-tipping, enhanced a focus on automatic behavior. Various studies reported on the divining rod, the
swinging pendulum, the planchette, and finally the ouija board late in
the century.

During this epoch, hypnosis was also undergoing another resurgence
of attention. While Azam was exploring its use in surgery and psychiatry, Durand de Gros published in 1860 a summary of the experience
and the studies of Braid, even suggesting the phenomena be renamed
Braidism. Auguste Ambroise Liébeault in Nancy used hypnosis from
1864 on and in 1866 his book appeared, but it would be nearly 20
years before it became well known. Hippolyte Bernheim fled from the
Alsace in 1871 to Nancy but did not become involved with Liébeault
until 1882. There his famous career in hypnotism was launched. In the
meantime, in Paris, Charcot was preparing to shift his focus from
organic neurological conditions (he was appointed Professor of Anatomy and Pathology in 1872) to those of a functional nature. Partly
inspired by Charles Richet's work, Charcot started investigating hypnosis and its connection with hysteria in 1878 and by 1882 gave his
famous paper to the Académie des Sciences. Soon Charcot would be
teaching two young and relatively unknown students who would contribute so much to dissociation and allied topics, Sigmund Freud and
Pierre Janet.[31]

As a poignant ending to this account, we may recall that in July
1880, a bright and educated young woman of 20 started to nurse her
dying father. Like the shamans before her, she had to grapple with the
spectre of death and in her own fashion, she developed a creative illness.
Her symptoms were myriad, but many had to do with changes in her
consciousness (including "absences," clear-cut trances) and splits in her
memory, including the loss of an entire language. At one point her
current personality disappeared and another took its place: in this case
it was herself but existing a year before in a state in which she lived

without any apparent awareness of what had happened to her in the interim. It is this case of Anna O. and her doctor, Josef Breuer, who become important to the next epoch in our review and who had so much to do in inspiring the studies that followed.[32]

Clinical observations had raised many questions by 1880 about the range of phenomena observed and the factors that made them possible in cases of multiple personality, spontaneous trances, trances induced by the varying techniques of hypnotism, and changes in consciousness produced by drugs. Of the various explanations offered, we have focused on the evolution of psychological hypotheses, especially those leading to dissociation. Topics that emerged and set the stage for the immense growth of psychological speculations at the turn of the nineteenth century included amnesia, reflex ideas, the continued association of energy with ideas both subconscious and unconscious, and the concept of the pathogenic idea or secret. From this mixture emerged the stress on unresolved issues in the unconscious which led to symptoms and illness. The ramifications of multiple personalities would lead to proposals of dédoublement by Azam in 1876, to Janet's repetition of this term as well as use of dissociation and disaggregation from 1886–1888, to Freud's discussion of dissociation in 1892 (but for Freud, "splitting" was a more popular word), and to the writings of Morton Prince from 1885 on. The struggle for understanding continues to the present day.

Notes

1. Jess Stein, ed., *The Random House Dictionary of the English Language.* New York: Random House, 1967.
2. Eric T. Carlson, "The History of Multiple Personality in the United States: Mary Reynolds and Her Subsequent Reputation," *Bulletin of the History of Medicine* 58 (1984): 72–82.
3. Mircea Eliade, *Shamanism: Archaic Techniques of Ecstasy.* Princeton: Princeton University Press, 1964. All our discussion of shamanism is based on this important work.
4. Adolf Rodewyk, *Possessed by Satan: The Church's Teaching on the Devil, Possession, and Exorcism.* Garden City, N.Y.: Doubleday, 1975, pp. 65–93.
5. Meribeth M. Simpson and Eric T. Carlson, "The Strange Sleep of Rachel Baker," *The Academy Bookman* 21 (1968): 2–13.
6. Eric T. Carlson and Meribeth M. Simpson, "Tarantism or Hysteria? An

American Case of 1801," *Journal of the History of Medicine* 26 (1971): 293–302.

7. Eric T. Carlson, "Jane C. Rider and Her Somnambulistic Vision," *Histoire des Sciences Médicales* 17 (1982) (special number 2): 110–114.

8. Alexandre Bertrand, *Traité du Somnambulisme.* Paris: Dentu, 1823; and *Du Magnétisme Animal en France.* Paris: Baillière, 1826. See Eric J. Dingwall, *Abnormal Hypnotic Phenomena. I: France.* New York: Barnes & Noble, 1968, pp. 46–54.

9. Richard Hunter and Ida Macalpine, *Three Hundred Years of Psychiatry: 1535–1860.* London: Oxford University Press, 1963, pp. 174–177.

10. Eberhardt Gmelin, *Materialen für die Anthropologie.* Tübingen: Cotta, 1791, pp. 3–89. Eric T. Carlson, "The History of Multiple Personality in the United States, I. The Beginnings," *American J. Psychiatry* 138 (1981): 666–668.

11. Robert I. Watson, *The Great Psychologists: From Aristotle to Freud.* Philadelphia: Lippincott, 1963, pp. 58–60, 164–166, 175–176, 186–189.

12. Erasmus Darwin, *Zoonomia; or, the Laws of Organic Life,* 2 vols. Dublin: Byrne & Jones, 1794–1796. I, pp. 232–234, 243, 42, 240, 214–221.

13. Darwin, ibid. I, pp. 240–246, 481, 493–494.

14. Thomas Beddoes, *Hygëia; Or Essays Moral and Medical on the Causes Affecting the Personal State of Our Middling and Affluent Classes,* 3 vols. Bristol: Phillips, 1802–1803. II, essay 9, pp. 90, 64, 72, 184, 86; essay 10, p. 21.

15. Eric T. Carlson, Jeffrey L. Wollock and Patricia S. Noel, eds., *Benjamin Rush's Lectures on the Mind.* Philadelphia: American Philosophical Society, 1981, pp. 489–493. Henceforth cited as *LOM.*

16. Benjamin Rush, *Medical Inquiries upon the Diseases of the Mind.* Philadelphia: Kimber & Richardson, 1812, pp. 259–262. Henceforth cited as *DOM.*

17. George W. Corner, ed., *The Autobiography of Benjamin Rush.* Princeton: Princeton University Press, 1948, pp. 93, 242. Rush, *DOM,* p. 277.

18. Rush, *DOM,* p. 165.

19. Rush, *LOM,* pp. 669–670.

20. Franklin Fearing, *Reflex Action: A Study in the History of Physiological Psychology.* Baltimore: Williams & Wilkins, 1930.

21. Thomas Laycock, "On the Reflex Function of the Brain," *British and Foreign Medical Review* 19 (1845): 298–311. Henceforth cited as *Reflex.* For my understanding of Laycock and Carpenter, I have relied heavily on the excellent unpublished doctoral dissertation by Roger Smith, "Physiological Psychology and the Philosophy of Nature in Mid-Nineteenth Century Britain," University of Cambridge, King's College, 1970. I appreciate greatly his research and that Dr. Smith shared his copy of the dissertation with me. See particularly pp. 1–130.

22. Smith, ibid., p. 77. Laycock, *Reflex,* pp. 301–302, 309.

23. Laycock, *Reflex,* pp. 303, 313, 308.

24. Smith, "Physiological Psychology," pp. 100–118.
25. Thomas Laycock, "On Certain Organic Disorders and Defects of Memory," *Edinburgh Medical Journal* (April 1874), abstracted by James Maclaren in *Journal of Mental Science* 20 (1874): 307–309.
26. Thomas Laycock, "A Chapter on some Organic Laws of Personal and Ancestral Memory," *Journal of Mental Science* 21 (1875): 155–187.
27. In addition, Laycock also spoke of the conservation values of some of the automatic actions of the body and that certain lower species passed these characteristics on to their offspring in a consistent fashion. Even though they were rudimentary in man, they still could act when proper circumstances allowed their stimulation. Laryngeal closure was one of these. Without stressing amphibians as such, Laycock appears to have made his point in 1845 also.
28. Stanley W. Jackson, "The History of Freud's Concept of Regression," *Journal of the American Psychoanalytic Association* 17 (1969): 743–784.
29. Kenneth Levin, *Freud's Early Psychology of the Neuroses: A Historical Perspective*. Pittsburgh: University of Pittsburgh Press, 1978, pp. 22–23. Henri F. Ellenberger, *The Discovery of the Unconscious*. New York: Basic Books, 1970, pp. 241–242, 289, 311–312.
30. Etienne Eugène Azam, *Hypnotisme, Double Conscience et Altérations de la Personnalité*. Paris: Baillière, 1887.
31. Leon Chertok and Raymond de Saussure, *The Therapeutic Revolution: From Mesmer to Freud*. New York: Brunner/Mazel, 1979. Ellenberger, *Discovery*, pp. 88–101, 124–126, 143–145. See also Georges Guillain, *J.-M. Charcot (1825–1893): His Life—His Work*. New York: Hocker, 1959.
32. Josef Breuer and Sigmund Freud, *Studies in Hysteria*. New York: Basic Books, 1957, pp. 21–47.

2. The Lure of Nonmaterialism in Materialist Europe: Investigations of Dissociative Phenomena, 1880–1915

Hannah S. Decker, Ph.D.

Introduction: The Two Faces of Science

Scientific investigation has long been artificially divided into two basic varieties. One kind is based on a materialistic approach. It is organically and laboratory-oriented and attached to experimentation and quantification. The other type of scientific investigation is founded on a nonmaterialistic approach. It is not directed toward studying physical objects or bodily parts and is conducted outside of laboratories. It relies on subjective accounts and verbal communications. Since the seventeenth century, both scientific approaches have existed side by side, but the materialist variety has been and remains dominant.

Periodically, the nonmaterialist approach attains a certain momentum and strength. While at those times it does not replace the materialist outlook, it has such vigorous proponents and becomes so noticeable, that for a number of years it is a simultaneous scientific theme and even gives the appearance of being dominant. Rarely have materialist and nonmaterialistic science coalesced, although such union has been the goal of select nineteenth- and twentieth-century thinkers. The artificial dichotomy still prevails—two faces of science, as it were. This means that until a unified scientific approach is achieved, scholars have to study the history of scientific subjects as a story of disparate and competing material and nonmaterial approaches.

At the end of the nineteenth and beginning of the twentieth century, there was a considerable upsurge of interest in nonmaterialist phenomena. The subjects that drew strong scrutiny were nonmaterial presence and spirit communication, hypnotism, multiple personality, altered states of consciousness, and the existence of unconscious ideas. On the one hand, the scientific curiosity about and study of dissociative phenomena were a reaction to the failures of the materialist science of the day, to the impact of Darwinism, and to the decline of religious faith. On the other hand, the interest in dissociation was also a renewed exploration of already existing knowledge. In many cases, the new inquiries attempted to combine nineteenth-century scientific methods with long-standing interests in dissociative phenomena. Along with the scientific and medical concerns with dissociation, there commenced a literary preoccupation with the complexity and disunity of the human personality which has continued up to the present. But a great deal of the scientific interest diminished around the time of the First World War.

Mirabile dictu, the year 1882 stands forth as the opening of an era. In 1882, the Society for Psychical Research was founded in London. Led by Frederic W. H. Myers (1843–1901), the Society grew out of the interests of a group of young Cambridge scholars in the varied phenomena of spiritism. In the same year, the celebrated neurologist, Jean-Martin Charcot (1835–1893), delivered his paper "On the Various Nervous States Determined by the Hypnosis of Hysterics" before the French Academy of Sciences in Paris.[1] Thereupon hypnotism, long neglected or derided, received instant respectability. Also in Paris, five months later, Pierre Janet (1859–1947), soon to win fame as a psychologist, received his *Agrégation de Philosophie* from the *Ecole Normale.* He immediately began his teaching career and thought of writing his doctoral thesis on hallucinations as a means of studying human perception.[2] Meanwhile, in the east of France, a country physician, A. A. Liébeault (1823–1904), was building a reputation for his miraculous cures using hypnosis. It was in 1882 that Liébeault was visited by a nearby professor of internal medicine, Hippolyte Bernheim (1840–1919), who was converted to his ideas.[3] Finally, in Vienna, in November 1882, Josef Breuer (1842–1925), the much-esteemed internist, told Sigmund Freud (1856–1939), then a resident, about his hypnotic treatment of Anna O.[4]

The Neo-Romanticist Reaction

What prompted such a dramatic eruption of activity? It is a question worth asking because only twenty years later there were already signs of the ardor fading, and in ten more years the scientific enthusiasm for spiritist phenomena and hypnotism had almost spent itself. I have already stated that interest in dissociative phenomena took place as a subordinate development, in a scientific Europe that was oriented toward naturalism and materialism, and the interest was in part a reaction to that preponderant viewpoint. Figures like Nietzsche, Dostoevsky, and Ibsen were representative of this rebellion of the 1880s against a world that stressed manifest appearance. Friedrich Nietzsche (1844–1900) wanted psychology to reveal the true nature of people as self-deceiving and also constantly deceiving others. Since a person lies to himself, the psychologist, he argued, has to be able to draw conclusions from what the person really means, rather than from what he says or even does. Nietzsche claimed that when the Gospel says, "He that humbles himself shall be exalted," what was really meant was "He that humbles himself wishes to be exalted."[5] If not actually self-deception, all feelings, opinions, and conduct are rooted in unconscious lies. Thus, the unconscious is the essential part of personality; the conscious is a commentary on the unconscious.

Nietzsche was part of a widespread neo-Romanticism in European life. This could be seen in some German and Austrian poets (Stefan George, Gerhart Hauptmann, Hugo von Hofmannsthal, and Rainer Maria Rilke); in the Symbolists in France, whose poetic inspiration came from the Swedenborgian belief that visible realities are symbols for the invisible world of the spirit[6] (the movement's leaders were Stéphane Mallarmé, Paul Verlaine, and Charles Baudelaire); and in the *Jugendstil* art movement in Germany. To some extent, the spirit of decadence and fin-de-siècle was the culmination of neo-Romanticism. Where industrialized Europe was optimistic, the neo-Romantics, seeing the artificiality of life, were pessimistic. It is in this context that one should view Max Nordau's 1892 book *Degeneration,* a well-received critique of contemporary culture. In keeping with this pessimism, Morel's theory of "mental degeneration" was widely implemented in French psychiatry of the 1880s by Valentin Magnan. Almost all patients' diagnoses in French mental hospitals were listed as "mental degeneracy with [the specific symptoms]."[7] Where the majority celebrated bigness and joint effort, the neo-Romantics idealized the individual. Like the Romantics before them, they were preoccupied with the irrational. They often pursued a mysticism that led to religious conversion or the joining of spiritistic or occult sects. They had a heightened interest in hypnosis, somnambulism, dual and multiple personality, and mental illness, and the writers among them pursued these themes.

One of the most famous novels of hypnotism, of course, is George du Maurier's 1894 *Trilby,* with its hypnotist and music teacher, Svengali, who controlled Trilby's life. The subject of dual personality was classically portrayed in Oscar Wilde's *The Picture of Dorian Gray* (1890). In addition, the topics of somnambulism, crimes committed or forgotten while in an alternate state, hypnosis, dreams, and multiple personality were combined with each other in innumerable ways. For example, the 1908 novel, *Obsession: Myself and the Other,* was based on documents collected at the Salpêtrière and concerns a painter who cannot rid himself of a second personality that sometimes takes over and damages his normal life. Finally, he is cured by a doctor who suggests to him the death and burial of the alternate personality. The Nobel prize-winning physiologist, Charles Richet (1850–1935), a pioneer in the scientific study of hypnotism, wrote a novel (1889), under a pseudonym, about a young physician who hypnotizes an orphan girl about to take her vows as a nun. In the hypnotic state, another personality appears who turns out to be in love with the doctor as well as the heiress to a great fortune. The couple are about to elope when the nun personality reappears and takes her vows. *The Somnambulist* (1880) told the story of an upstanding Protestant minister who, unbeknownst to his awake self, becomes a criminal in his somnambulistic state, raping women and killing children. In *The Other* (1893) by Paul Lindau, a judge discovers that he, in an alternate personality, is really the perpetrator of the crime he is investigating. I cannot, of course, leave this catalogue without mentioning Robert Louis Stevenson's 1886 classic, *The Strange Case of Dr. Jekyll and Mr. Hyde.* Stevenson said he got the idea for the book from "little people" who came to him in his dreams.[8]

I must also add that there was an obvious affinity between the patients in contemporary case histories and the characters in the works of the literary masters of the age. For example, Janet's famous patient, the 23-year-old Irène, who in 1900 succumbed to hysterical disturbances, somnambulistic crises, hallucinations, and amnesia after her mother's death, is strikingly similar to Pauline in Emile Zola's (1840–1902) *La Joie de Vivre* of 1884. Hofmannsthal's (1874–1929) character Elektra (1909) can be compared with Breuer's Anna O., while Freud's Dora would fit very well in a short story by Arthur Schnitzler (1862–1931).

These often lurid stories illustrate a preoccupation with the sensational, but as time passed, more subtle literary themes developed, along with more sophisticated scientific knowledge about variations in personality that were not as dramatic as split personality. In a sense, these literary and scientific concerns already show the withdrawal from the high-water mark of dissociative phenomena at the beginning of the twentieth century. For example, Marcel Prévost's (1862–1941) *The Secret Garden* (1897) deals with a married woman who becomes aware of her unmarried personality. She awakens to all kinds of new information, including the fact of her husband's infidelity. She goes through a long, inner struggle and ultimately elevates her married personality to a permanent level of heightened awareness. In this state, she decides to stay with her husband rather than leave him.[9] Furthermore, a new literary device appeared: the "inner monologue," foreshadowing the stream of consciousness. For example, Schnitzler's short novel, *Lieutenant Gustl* (1901), has no particular action, only a description of the character's thoughts.[10]

One also sees subtle descriptions of the many facets of human personality and their interplay in the early twentieth-century works of Luigi Pirandello (1867–1936), Marcel Proust (1871–1922), James Joyce (1882–1941), and Virginia Woolf (1882–1941). These authors share an interest in the unconscious in its many manifestations, no longer primarily emphasizing the obvious aspects of unconscious phenomena as seen in hypnotism and dual personality. They have left the stark dichotomies of awake vs. hypnotized, or Personality A vs. Personality B. They are dealing with *multiplicity* in personality rather than the flagrant *multiple* personality, yet with a recognition that illness and bizarreness can still be present in the more muted manifestation. Proust, for instance, mentions only one clear-cut case of dual personality. He was interested instead in the many facets of personality in all of us. Personality changes from moment to moment, depending on place, time, and our companions. There is no one "real" ego, but rather a succession of egos, or the alternating dominance of different aspects of the ego. Virginia Woolf in *The Waves* (1931) has her character Bernard say: "I am not one person; I am many people."[11]

The Unconscious Mind

All the above describes some major elements in the European intellectual climate that partly paved the way for and partly accompanied scientific interest in unconscious and dissociative phenomena. Now I want to turn to the main aspects of the scientific developments. Out of a mass of material, I have chosen to emphasize spiritism, hypnotism, and the career of Pierre Janet. Janet's professional life is to a great extent the culmination of the history of the first scientific "rise and fall" of dissociative phenomena. This is because he had contacts with scientific students of spiritism; he was a frequent and successful utilizer of hypnotism; he insisted on applying scientific methods to his inquiries; he coined the words "subconscious" and "dissociation"; and his personal influence diminished at the same time as general scientific interest in dissociative occurrences (especially that of multiple personality) declined. The extent to which the overall attention to dissociation was affected by Janet's waning reputation is not clear and could be the subject of further discussion. At any rate, rather arbitrarily and somewhat artificially, I will discuss in turn spiritism, hypnotism, Janet, and the failure of dissociation to maintain itself as a major scientific concern in the first half of the twentieth century.

First, however, one introductory note is necessary. Before the Western world could consider the workings of the human mind on a scientific basis, the beliefs in possession by spirits and in exorcism through magic or religious rituals had to be surrendered. This happened somewhat dramatically at the end of the eighteenth century when exorcism and hypnosis had a fateful confrontation. A Catholic priest, Father Johann Joseph Gassner (1727–1779) had acquired a considerable reputation for healing people, including himself, of a wide variety of ills by using the Church's rituals of exorcism. But there was also much opposition to Gassner because of Enlightenment thought that considered Church practices to be magical and irrational. Prince Max Joseph of Bavaria appointed a commission of inquiry in 1775 and invited Franz Anton Mesmer (1734–1815), an Austrian physician, to show that the results of exorcism could also be obtained by the so-called "natural" methods of animal magnetism. Mesmer produced the same effects as Gassner: he caused convulsions and cured them. Gassner was dispatched to be a priest in a small community. Pope Pius VI ordered his own investigation and concluded "that exorcism was to be performed only with discretion. . . . [Thus] it was only with the decline of the widespread belief in possession that personality disturbances came into the realm of medical science: hence fugues and multiple personalities as we know them are largely a post-Mesmer set of phenomena."[12]

Thus, occurrences of divided personality appeared at the end of the eighteenth century. The first one was reported by Eberhardt Gmelin in 1791 as a case of "exchanged personality" (*umgetauschte Persönlichkeit*) and concerned a young German woman with a secondary aristocratic French personality. Through hypnosis, Gmelin was able to make her shift from one personality to another.[13] Partly because of this growth of knowledge of multiple personality, a new model of the mind developed during the early nineteenth century: the mind was dual; there were conscious and unconscious mental states. Later, it was said that there was a dominant conscious personality with a group of underlying subpersonalities. Eventually, it was declared that split fragments of personality could act autonomously.

Spiritism and Parapsychology

Knowledge about the workings of the unconscious mind was also considerably enhanced by the popular wave of spiritualism that began to spread over Europe in the 1850s. Although the fad originated in the United States, it received an impetus in Europe from the psychological manifestations that accompanied and followed the revolutions of 1848. A French commentator on the "moving tables and the rapping spirits" that excited the public imagination wrote in 1856: "In our epoch of revolutions, considerable upheavals often disturb society, filling some with profound fears, others with unlimited hope. The nervous system has become more sensitive. . . . Such are the circumstances which favoured the contemporary explosion."[14] Europeans discovered that the spiritist manifestations depended on the personalities of the participants. The most effective individuals were the "mediums" who could act as intermediaries between the living and the dead. Some mediums could write automatically, speak in a trance, and allegedly produce physical phenomena. By the 1860s spirits were manifesting themselves visually during seances. The epidemic slowly receded, but many spiritist groups remained active, publishing pamphlets and journals, and holding congresses. "Many Mesmerists were among the first and most active supporters of the new movement."[15] Sometimes a believer in spiritism founded a lay religion.

Gradually, a new science of parapsychology emerged. Spiritism provided psychologists and psychopathologists with new approaches to the mind. Automatic writing and gazing into mirrors, crystal balls, and water were taken over by scientists as methods of exploring the unconscious. Sometimes the investigators studied mediums, and sometimes they studied hysterical persons or individuals with multiple personalities. Two of the special instruments devised for communicating with the spirits via automatic writing received wide attention. One was the planchette which first appeared in France c. 1853–56. It was a little heart-shaped table, seven inches by five inches. The planchette stood on three legs, one of which was actually a sharpened lead pencil slipped into a rubber socket at the tip. The other two legs were mounted on casters so the whole board could move freely in any direction over the paper on which it wrote. The second instrument was the ouija board. Its name was based on "yes-yes" in French and German, although it was invented in Baltimore in 1890. Like the planchette, it served both for parlor games and as a means of communication with departed spirits.

A wide variety of scientists became intrigued and sometimes duped by mediums. In 1871, one of the Fox sisters who had started the epidemic in the United States, convinced Sir William Crookes, inventor of the Crookes vacuum tube and a renowned chemist and physicist, that the sounds heard by the sisters "were true objective occurrences not produced by trickery or mechanical means."[16] Alfred Russel Wallace (1823–1913), the discoverer along with Charles Darwin of natural selection, studied and experimented with spiritualism beginning in the late 1860s and became a firm believer. His additional essays on natural selection published in 1870 contended "that man has not, like the other animals, been produced by the unaided operation of natural selection, but that other forces have also been in operation."[17] In 1874 Wallace wrote that since adolescence he had been totally irreligious and still remained so. But his "thorough and confirmed . . . materialist" beliefs had been overcome "by the continuous action of fact after fact" so that he had been "led . . . to accept Spiritualism."[18] Arthur Conan Doyle (1859–1930), a physician as well as the creator of the superobservant Sherlock Holmes, also became a spiritualist and a lecturer and writer on spiritualism.[19]

Other scientists used the spiritist craze as a point of embarkation for critical, though not necessarily unsympathetic, investigation of the unconscious mind. By 1880, many philosophers admitted the existence of unconscious mental life, relying heavily on the conceptions of Arthur Schopenhauer (1788–1860) and Eduard von Hartmann (1842–1906).[20] Already Michel-Eugène Chevreul in 1833 and 1854 had written that movements of the "spirits" were really the result of unconscious muscular movements of the subject or medium caused by unconscious thoughts.[21] But the best-known parapsychological research had its origins in Cambridge in the 1870s with the intent of determining whether clairvoyance, foreknowledge of the future, and purported communication with the dead were indeed possible. The men involved eventually banded together in the Society for Psychical Research. They included William Barrett, a physicist, the Reverend Stainton Moses, a clergyman, Henry Sidgwick, a philosopher, Edmund Gurney, a psychologist, and Frank Podmore, a civil servant. Frederic Myers, a classical scholar, was the leading figure in the Society until his death in 1901.

Myers asked the question: "Is the Universe friendly?"[22] To know the answer, reasoned Myers, one had first to find out if there is life beyond the grave. Therefore, the issue of survival after death came to be the main concern of the Society's research. In investigating this, Myers decided there had to be an analysis of hypnosis and dual personality. Only then could the question of communication with deceased spirits be answered. Myers examined all the literature dealing with these topics. This bibliographic search plus his and his colleagues' parapsychological research were gathered together in two large volumes entitled *Human Personality and Its Survival of Bodily Death*.[23] William James described the work as "the first attempt to consider the phenomena of hallucination, hypnotism, automatism, double personality and mediumship, as connected parts of one whole subject."[24] Myers called the unconscious mind the "subliminal self" and declared it had three functions. Its inferior functions were seen in the processes of dissociation. Its superior functions appeared in the works of genius which are actually the "subliminal uprush" of rich stores of information, feelings, and thoughts which lie beneath consciousness. It is through the superior functions of the unconscious mind that communication with the spirits of the deceased could occasionally occur. Finally, there was the mythopoeic function, which was the unconscious tendency to create fantasies.

Myers and Edmund Gurney investigated the use of the planchette in nonmediumistic settings and collected numerous anecdotes on its working. They decided its productions probably came from the unconscious mind, rather than being received telepathically (through thought transference) or from spirits. Nevertheless, in keeping with their conception of the superior functions of the unconscious mind, they considered that the planchette's automatic writing might come from spirits. The ouija board's workings could be explained like those of the planchette, and Myers observed that there could be automatic writing by pen alone. Frank Podmore, another early member of the Society, investigating physical phenomena such as table tilting, raps, mysterious lights, materialization, and the movement of objects without apparent normal contact, became increasingly skeptical and critical of mediums. He evaluated spiritualists' claims in his two-volume work, *Modern Spiritualism,* and later attempted to deal scientifically with the subject of mental and spiritual healing by tracing the origins of Christian Science to the practice of animal magnetism.[25]

The work of the Society for Psychical Research in the 1880s and 1890s constituted a transition from the mediumistic use of automatic writing to its clinical and experimental uses. Society members sought to determine if the unconscious or the spirits were at work in seemingly spontaneous, dissociated actions. Myers struggled to make a "dispassionate inquiry" into the subject of spiritualism, and this was admired by William James who became his good friend. When Myers lay dying, James sat outside his hospital room, hoping to catch "a message when Myers' spiritual self departed from his earthly body."[26]

Janet also studied spiritualist phenomena in the 1880s, but since I will deal with this in a separate section, I want to turn now to the research of Théodore Flournoy (1854–1920), physician, philosopher, psychologist, and disciple of the physiologic psychologist, Wilhelm Wundt (1832–1920). Flournoy was a professor of psychology at the University of Geneva and, under the influence of Wundt, sought to apply the techniques of experimental psychology to questions raised by parapsychology. He did a lengthy study of mediums in Geneva and in 1894 began to investigate intensively one medium, Hélène Smith. Her real name was Catherine Muller, and she was a 30-year-old saleswoman in a department store. She had a true belief in her spiritual powers and never took money for her mediumistic work. Flournoy studied Hélène Smith for five years, looking for a natural explanation of her spiritist activities. He found that as a child she had read a lot about the supposed other lives that she manifested. These were existences as a fifteenth-century Indian princess and as Marie Antoinette. She also claimed familiarity with life on Mars.

Flournoy published his study of Hélène Smith in 1900 under the title *From India to the Planet Mars*.[27] He showed that the medium's portrayals were really "a species of romance of the subliminal imagination" based on forgotten memories, which he called the "automatism of cryptomnesia." Her supposed other lives also expressed a wish to escape from the tedium of her everyday existence and job. The spirit who guided her, "Leopold," was actually her unconscious personality. Flournoy thought it a useful goal "to endeavor to fix the connections of mediumship with other functional affections of the nervous system. . . . Let us hope that a near future will establish some good mediums and their observers in [favorable] practical conditions . . . and that the day will come when the true place of mediumship in the framework of [neuropathological] nosology will be discovered."[28]

Flournoy's book raises for us today important ethical issues and indicates some of the problems faced by the new psychological sciences at the turn of the century. We generally think about these difficulties only in reference to Freud and forget that other researchers doing similar work became enmeshed in problems of confidentiality, transference, and even countertransference.

Edouard Claparède, the psychologist who wrote a biographical sketch about Flournoy, reported that Flournoy was aware of Hélène Smith's psychosexual attachment to him, but decided not to discuss it in his book in order not to embarrass her publicly.[29] However, the book still had great repercussions on her life. Flournoy showed that the "Martian" language the medium used had a French grammatical pattern, and a linguist who read the book pointed out that the vocabulary came from distorted Hungarian words. (Hélène Smith's father was Hungarian.) The upshot was that after a five-year intensive relationship, Hélène Smith broke with Flournoy; she also left the circle of her spiritist friends. A wealthy woman gave her an income so she did not have to work but could devote herself to being a medium. She left her job, thus severing her last links with reality, and lived out her life in almost total isolation.

To conclude this section, I should mention that Carl Gustav Jung

(1875–1961) based his doctoral dissertation on his two-year observation (1898–1900) of a teenage medium, Helene Preiswerk, who was his cousin. Published in 1902 under the title of *On the Psychology and Pathology of So-Called Occult Phenomena,* the dissertation dealt with his cousin's somnambulistic states, her second personality, her talking in an unknown language, her automatic writing, her journeys to Mars, her past lives, and other hallucinatory phenomena.[30]

Hypnotism and Multiple Personality

The parapsychological movement which began in the 1860s and 1870s played a role in the revival of interest in hypnotism, although such interest had never died out completely, either in England or on the Continent. Indeed, the existence of several generations of magnetizers and hypnotists had resulted in the slow development of a dynamic psychiatry in the nineteenth century and the creation of a store of knowledge about unconscious psychological occurrences. Through hypnotism, various psychopathological conditions were explored: spontaneous somnambulism, lethargy, catalepsy, multiple personality, and hysteria.[31]

The problem that must be specifically addressed is why there was a dramatic rebirth of interest in hypnotism just around 1880, aside from whatever impact spiritism had. References to the *Zeitgeist* as a causal explanation—although there is much substantiating evidence—will provide only a partial answer because it is a form of the chicken and egg question, i.e., which came first—the "spirit of the times" or the enthusiasm for hypnotism? I think the answer has to be sought primarily in the growing awareness of multiple personality coupled with the gradual growth of knowledge about unconscious phenomena.

The first objective study of multiple personality appeared in 1840. It concerned the case of "Estelle," an 11-year-old girl who suffered extreme pain. A physician, Despine, magnetized her. After a month she developed two personalities. Eventually the two personalities merged and she got better.[32] Despine wrote a book about his success, and we know that Janet was later inspired by it. As more and more cases of multiple personality were published, it was seen that they fell into some general groups. A very rare category was that of simultaneously existing multiple personalities. Such a situation never lasted too long. More usual was the category of successive multiple personalities, divided into a few subgroups. For example, the personalities could be mutually aware of each other, although one was dominant. Or, the personalities could be mutually unaware of each other. Or there could be awareness only in one direction, i.e., Tom doesn't know George, but George knows himself and Tom. One of the most famous cases of this type was that of Félida X., who was first treated in 1858 by Eugène Azam (1822–1899), a professor of surgery in Bordeaux interested in hypnotism.[33] Most cases involved awareness in one direction, and usually the personality who appeared second was freer and gayer than the first personality who was inhibited and depressed. This fact led Myers and then Janet to declare that it was therefore incorrect to call the first personality normal and the second personality abnormal. The first personality was actually the sick one, and the second might be considered a return to a former, healthy self.

The more reports appeared on multiple personality, the more cases were recognized and reported. And as this happened, the cases described became increasingly complex. The reports had started out as descriptions of short fugue states followed by amnesia; they ended up as prolonged, complicated, and mysterious cases of multiple personalities. Moreover, an increased number of psychological phenomena were defined as representing or exhibiting aspects of multiple personality, e.g., depersonalization.

Over the years, information was gathered about multiple personality and its relation to hypnosis. To wit: There could be a whole set of personalities; under hypnosis a third personality could appear. The investigator himself, consciously or unconsciously, could prompt the multiplication and development of personalities. If an unconscious personality adopted or was given a name, it showed itself more clearly. Hypnosis could produce age regression. A controversy ensued over whether this was true regression or an excellent imitation. In hypnosis, there was a loss or modification of voluntary control. Did this mean that a person could be made to commit a seduction or a crime?

The 1875 publication by the physiologist Charles Richet of a scholarly paper on "induced somnambulism" renewed the possibility of scientific research on hypnotism.[34] It was probably Richet who influenced Charcot to start investigating hypnotism around 1878. Richet was one of several physicians who began to reconsider their attitudes toward hypnotism after seeing impressive performances by traveling stage hypnotists such as Hansen in Germany and Donato in Belgium, France, and Italy.[35] There arose two schools of hypnotism which made great contributions. One was at Nancy under Bernheim, who, since he was a professor of medicine at the university, was able to lend legitimacy to his investigations. Bernheim had wide influence throughout Europe, affecting the work of Albert Moll and Alfred von Schrenck-Notzing in Germany, Richard von Krafft-Ebing and Sigmund Freud in Austria, Vladimir Bechterev in Russia, Milne Bramwell in England, Boris Sidis and Morton Prince in the United States, Otto Wetterstrand in Sweden, Frederick Van Eeden and A. W. von Renterghem in Holland, and August Forel in Switzerland.

Forel (1848–1931) deserves special mention because it is often not realized how far-reaching was his commitment to the use of hypnosis. He started out as an organicist but gradually changed his orientation, troubled by such observations that a psychiatrist could not cure alcoholics but a layman could. After he signed a pledge to abstain from alcohol, he discovered his success rate with alcoholic patients increased markedly. This caused him to realize that effective psychotherapy was partly the result of the personal attitude of the therapist. His training in hypnotism in 1888 under Bernheim at Nancy was another step in learning about the efficacy of psychotherapy. The next year he published a textbook on hypnotism and its relation to suggestion and psychotherapy.[36] Then, as head of the Burghölzli mental hospital, he organized an out-patient service where hypnosis was used to treat patients with physical ailments. Eugen Bleuler (1857–1939) and Adolf Meyer (1866–1950) were both his students.

The other school of hypnotism was at the Salpêtrière hospital, led by the neurologist Charcot. His career is especially significant because of the way he brought together the studies of hysteria and hypnotism. In 1870, at the age of 35, Charcot was one of the chief physicians at the Salpêtrière and in charge of a special ward for women suffering from convulsions. He began to distinguish between hysterical and epileptic convulsions and to investigate hysteria. Then came his initial probings into hypnotism which resulted in his deciding that there were three stages in a hysterical patient's hypnotic trance: lethargy, catalepsy, and finally somnambulism. In 1882 he gave his celebrated paper on hypnotism before the French Academy, and two years later he was able to reproduce hysterical paralyses under hypnosis. Charcot achieved great personal fame and had a reputation (falsely, of course) as the man who had discovered hysteria, hypnotism, dual personality, catalepsy, and somnambulism. He was known as the "Napoleon of Neuroses." Charcot had a great impact on writers of his day because he revealed to many of them unsuspected realms of the mind. He influenced Alphonse Daudet and his son Léon Daudet, Zola, Guy de Maupassant, Joris-Karl Huysmans, Paul Bourget, Pirandello, and Proust.[37]

In addition to the impetus given hypnotism by the increasing incidence of multiple personality, psychiatrists and neurologists looked to hypnotism to provide the cure for pressing new psychiatric illnesses. Challenged by the high incidence of neurasthenia, alcoholism, hysteria, phobias, anxiety neurosis, and traumatic neurosis, official medicine was on the lookout for new theories and new therapies. Could hypnosis be a solution to the problems of nineteenth-century neuroses? It seemed to be a powerful tool because of the control the hypnotist exerted over the behavior of his subject. This control was explained by William James on the basis of "ideomotor action."[38] Although James named the concept, which is still used today, the principle that the idea is the direct instigator of action has strong European roots. The Scottish philosopher, Alexander Bain (1818–1903), propounded his "law of diffusion" in 1859, i.e., every sensory or emotional feeling has its movement consequences. The idea was restated by Charles Féré (1852–1907) in 1887 as the concept of "dynamogenesis": muscular action is increased by sensory stimulation.[39] Bernheim also used it in his theory of suggestion under the rubric of the "law of ideodynamism": "any suggested and accepted idea tends to turn into acts."[40]

In sum, in the 1880s and into the 1890s confidence in hypnotism and suggestion was high. They were invoked to explain many historical and sociological phenomena such as the genesis of religions, belief in miracles, the existence of wars, and crowd psychology (cf. Gustave Le Bon's work of 1895).[41] New educational theories were also based on suggestion. I have already discussed the novels which were inspired. Hypnotism and multiple personality impressed philosophers and psychologists, especially Frenchmen like Hippolyte Taine (1828–1893) who wrote on intelligence, Théodule Ribot (1839–1916) who was concerned with diseases of memory and personality, and Henri Bergson (1859–1941) who participated personally in hypnotic sessions.[42] Janet wrote that the report Azam published in 1887 about his patient, Félida, was instrumental in the establishment of a chair of psychology at the Collège de France.[43]

The existence of multiple personality led especially English and French thinkers to conclude that literary, artistic, and scientific creativity was the coming into consciousness of an alternate personality or the eruption of subconscious material. Flournoy also used his notion of cryptomnesia to explain literary creation and some cases of literary plagiarism.[44] Jung, too, explained a famous case of literary plagiarism on the basis of cryptomnesia.[45]

Dissociation and Pierre Janet

It was from repeated dealing with cases of multiple personality in clinical situations that physicians and psychologists began to formulate a notion of dissociation. Already Puységur and the early magnetists pointed out that the hypnotized person, while under hypnosis, is living a special life with its own continuity, separate from his normal conscious life. Over the course of the nineteenth century, the concept of the double ego began to develop. The magnetizers and hypnotists saw a second personality emerge with a life of its own and wondered how two minds could coexist simultaneously and what their relation was to each other. Many investigators said the second mind contained forgotten memories of events, daydreams, and fantasies which followed an autonomous development independent of the conscious mind. This theory was developed by Max Dessoir (1867–1947), who after he compiled a large bibliography on contemporary hypnotism, wrote *The Double Ego*.[46] His formulation was that the mind consists of two layers, each with its own complex chain of associations. There was the "upper consciousness" (*Oberbewusstsein*) and the "lower consciousness" (*Unterbewusstsein*). Hypnosis summons up the lower consciousness. It is within this context that Pierre Janet, as a young man in his mid-twenties, framed the idea of *désagrégations psychologiques* (psychological dissociations).

Pierre Janet was born in 1859 and educated at the Ecole Normale Supérieure along with other greats such as Henri Bergson.[47] Like many young philosophers of his time, he was influenced by Charcot's 1882 paper on hypnosis. He also discussed neuroses and hypnotism with his brother, Jules, who was a medical student. While a teacher at a high school in Le Havre, he worked as a volunteer at the hospital and conducted psychiatric research on his own. It was when he was searching for a suitable topic for his doctoral thesis that he learned about a 45-year-old woman, Léonie, who could be hypnotized from a distance, i.e., she was telepathic.[48] Starting in 1885, Janet carried out a number of experiments on Léonie and published papers describing his observations. One paper was read at the Society of Physiological Psychology in Paris by Janet's uncle, a well-known philosopher, and greatly impressed the audience, including Charcot. As a result Richet and a delegation from the Society for Psychical Research came to Le Havre to observe Léonie. Janet's results were confirmed, and Janet acquired immediate fame in those scientific circles involved in spiritist and hypnotic investigations. But Janet eschewed any involvement with parapsychology and decided to devote himself only to research on hypnosis and suggestion. He also discovered that Léonie had been hypnotized in the past; her present displays were repetitions of old magnetic sessions. This fostered his desire to see only fresh patients in order to ensure the best experimental results.

Janet's doctoral dissertation, *Psychological Automatism* (1889), was based on 27 patients he had seen during the four previous years.[49] Influenced by the experimental psychologist Ribot to use rigorous methods, he had instituted strict procedures, which he continued to observe. He examined all patients without there being others in the room who could affect the results. He recorded exactly whatever the patients said or did. And he studied carefully life histories and past treatments. Janet said nothing in his book about the parapsychological experiment with Léonie, but concentrated on three other women of whom Lucie, age 19, is an example: Lucie was overcome by attacks of terror without apparent reason. Using automatic writing, Janet found the cause and meaning of her attacks. When she was seven, two men hiding behind a curtain had frightened her as a practical joke. Lucie had no awareness of this episode, but a second personality, Adrienne, had, and was emerging and reliving the frightening event. At these times, Lucie had her panics.

Janet divided psychological automatism into two large categories. The first category was total automatism of the subject and included complete catalepsy, artificial somnambulism (the hypnotic state), and

"successive existences." (Janet avoided the term "alternating personalities.") The second category was partial automatism of the subject. In
this group, part of the personality was split off from self-awareness and
followed an independent, "subconscious" existence. Janet had originated the word "subconscious" to separate what he considered his
scientific-psychological approach from the metaphysical-philosophical
approach of von Hartmann, who used the word "unconscious." The
states ranked under partial automatism were: (1) partial catalepsy; (2)
distractions, e.g., an absentminded occurrence such as answering a
question unawares; (3) automatic writing, i.e., a person writing while
distracted and producing subconscious material; (4) posthypnotic suggestion, which Janet explained as the subconscious mind's persistence
into the waking state and attending to the carrying out of the hypnotist's commands.

What were all these "partially automatic" occurrences? Were they
indicative of simultaneous existences? Janet decided to call them "dissociations." He used the French word *désagrégations,* but by 1907 he
was accepting the English word, as can be seen by his Harvard lectures
published as *The Major Symptoms of Hysteria.*[50] The term "dissociation" became so common within a decade that Janet's name was no
longer used with it. Boris Sidis in 1902 used the words "disaggregation" and "dissociation" interchangeably.[51] "Dissociation" derived from
the doctrine of "association" which said that memories were brought to
consciousness by way of the association of ideas (e.g., the theories of
Richard Semon [1859–1918] and Eugen Bleuler). Therefore, the
memories not available to association were "disassociated." They were
split off from the major personality and existed as a subordinate personality, subconscious but capable of becoming represented in consciousness through hypnosis. Other dissociative phenomena that Janet said
were "partially automatic" included use of the divining rod, spiritism,
and mediumism, obsessive impulses, the fixed ideas and hallucinations
of psychotics, and possession, i.e., the individual is being controlled by
a subconscious idea, unknown to him or her, as in the case of Lucie.

Janet's dissertation gave him the reputation of an expert on hypnotism, and at the age of 30 he was one of a committee made up of
Liébeault, Bernheim, Déjerine, and Forel which led the International
Congress for Experimental and Therapeutic Hypnotism. He had experimentally confirmed much of the old knowledge of the magnetizers

and early hypnotists such as that when a secondary personality is identified and named—"baptized" as Janet put it—it tends to take on a clearer existence.[52] He had given added weight to the theory of ideomotor action by stating that it is the natural tendency of an idea to develop into an act; there is no sensation or feeling without movement. In his doctoral dissertation, in subsequent separate papers, and in his 1893 thesis for the M.D. degree,[53] he elaborated various theoretical positions. Much of the information was gathered first as a medical student on Charcot's wards and then, after Charcot's death in 1893, in a laboratory for experimental psychology at the Salpêtrière that Charcot's successor, Fulgence Raymond, allowed him to use. He also saw patients on the wards and at an outpatient clinic.

Underlying patients' dissociations, said Janet, there was always a weakness of the mind. Janet believed in mental degeneration over several generations, but did not think this was an inevitable, fated process, since diseases in families could recede. Nevertheless, mental disease in the individual who comes from a family where there is hereditary degeneracy may never go away completely. Hysterical patients suffered from the pathogenic role of "subconscious fixed ideas." The cause was usually a traumatic or frightening event that had become subconscious and had been replaced by symptoms. This replacement of a memory by a symptom was due to the narrowing of the field of consciousness which in turn was the result of the mental weakness. In short, "subconscious fixed ideas are both the result of mental weakness and a source of further and worse mental weakness."[54] Hysterical crises were often the disguised reenactment of subconscious fixed ideas. To look for the fixed ideas, Janet mainly used hypnosis. But he supplemented hypnosis with information from dreams, automatic writing, distraction, automatic talking (random talking aloud of the patient), and crystal gazing ("la divination par les miroirs.") Janet saw the hypnotic rapport as a kind of anesthesia, "a peculiar mode of perception . . . centered around the person of the hypnotist."[55] The rapport was another facet of the narrowing of the field of consciousness; it was a willed concentration upon the hypnotist and, therefore, not to be encouraged. When the rapport extended beyond the time of the hypnotic session, Janet called it "somnambulic influence" and sought to restrict it by seeing the patient at decreasing intervals.

In 1902, with the help of Bergson's endorsement, Janet got Ribot's position as professor of experimental psychology at the Collège de France; he beat out the psychologist Alfred Binet (1857–1911) for the job. His lecture topics, after several years, became less oriented toward psychopathology and clinical topics. Then, in 1910, Raymond died and was replaced at the Salpêtrière by J. J. Déjerine (1849–1917), a follower of Paul Dubois' (1848–1918) moral psychotherapy; Déjerine was hostile to Janet. Also Joseph Babinski (1857–1932), Charcot's former student, became more powerful. He was totally organically oriented and very suspicious of Janet who he felt was perpetuating Charcot's errors. Thus, on the eve of the first World War Janet was effectively forced out from the Salpêtrière.

It would not be right to leave the subject of Janet and dissociation without dwelling a moment on the prior work of Josef Breuer. Sometime in 1881 or 1882 Breuer came to the conclusion that

the splitting of consciousness . . . *is present* . . . *in every hysteria, and that a tendency to such a dissociation, and with it the emergence of abnormal states of consciousness* . . . *is the basic phenomenon of this neurosis.* . . . The basis and *sine qua non* of hysteria is the existence of hypnoid states. . . . The ideas which emerge in [hypnoid states] are very intense but are cut off from associative communication with the rest of the content of consciousness. . . . The nature of these states and the extent to which they are cut off from the remaining conscious processes must be supposed to vary . . . from complete recollection to total amnesia.

If hypnoid states of this kind are already present before the onset of the manifest illness, they provide the soil in which the affect plants the pathogenic memory with its consequent somatic phenomena. This corresponds to *dispositional* hysteria.

. . . These dispositional hypnoid states . . . often, it would seem, grow out of the day-dreams which are so common . . . and to which needlework and similar preoccupations render women especially prone.[56]

Breuer's theory as applied to the case of Anna O. meant that she was predisposed to a hypnoid state normally, or, while daydreaming, was in a light hypnoid state. When anxiety entered her life with the illness of her father, the hypnoid state was heightened and accompanied by amnesia. So there was a split, and her mind was divided into two parts, one where ideas never entered consciousness and one where ideas were conscious. This splitting occurred owing to a preparedness on Anna O.'s part, which was created by a kind of self-hypnosis.

Breuer's explanation for divided consciousness was different from the one Freud later evolved. Freud said the ideas unavailable to consciousness are in the unconscious because they have been repressed. Repressed ideas are bound up with affective impulses and enter consciousness only indirectly e.g., as physical symptoms. But Breuer's hypothesis was that the amnesia occurs because certain memories are not "usually available." The unavailable memories need not have any special affective or impulsive significance. The mind has just been divided into two parts on some basis, perhaps physiological or some combination of psychological and physiological.

At any rate, it is clear that Breuer had priority of discovery of dissociation, but Janet had priority of publication since Breuer did not publish until 1893. Although Breuer and Freud at first acknowledged Janet's claim,[57] the issue later became controversial and led to acrimony between Janet and the psychoanalysts.[58]

The Reassertion of Materialist Dominance

It is said with great regularity in studies about dissociation that the concept disappeared in the early years of the twentieth century. Freud's notion of repression became more popular than Breuer's idea of the hypnoid state and Janet's conception of the narrowing of the field of consciousness. Yet how many European psychiatrists and psychologists understood even Freud's theory? The point I wish to make is the one I set down at the beginning of this chapter. Why should concern with dissociation not have flagged? Why should there be any expectation that the interest in hypnotism, multiple personality, and manifestations of unconscious ideation should have persisted and flourished? The dominant scientific ideology remained materialistic. There had been reasons for the flowering of curiosity in and the reporting of dissociative occurrences, but not much had to happen for a decline to set in. This raises, by the way, a provocative issue. Is the existence of multiple personality, on the whole, iatrogenic? Do dual or multiple personalities mainly emerge under hypnosis? Without hypnosis, there is still pathology in the individual, of course, but would blatant personalities appear, or appear as frequently? I have no intention of attempting to answer these questions, but I raise them so that I, and you, do not become lulled into setting forth a simplistic scheme of the "rise and fall" of dissociation.

There was, of course a definite slackening of interest in dissociation and in some of its manifestations, and even though that does not surprise me, I do think it is worthwhile to explore the details of this. To begin with, it should be noted that there were psychologists, such as the experimentalists in Germany, who never investigated dissociation. The Wundtians were so determinedly "scientific" in the materialist sense that they did not even consider studying anything having to do with unconscious mental functioning. Nor did they believe they could deal with a concept of personality "scientifically." The personality was not amenable to introspection by scientific methods. Most academic psychologists in the late nineteenth and early twentieth centuries paid little attention to the topic of central regulatory mechanisms in the personality because they wanted to avoid asking whether there was a "will" prompting actions. The "will" was a taboo concept. Psychologists felt the question of volition was unscientific and "philosophic"; it would pull psychology back to its prescientific, mystical days. Instead, psychologists preferred to think in terms of "habits."[59] The Würzburg school briefly introduced notions such as "sets" or "determining tendencies" to account for certain nonmeasurable aspects of the subject's response, but these were stamped out as equally "unscientific" by Wundt before World War I.

In other words, the psychologists refused to deal with anything that resembled a "soul" or the "unconscious," i.e., any nonmaterial, nondemonstrable, central explanatory mechanism for human behavior. Instead, they substituted "a hierarchy of possible thoughts and actions determined by the competitive strengths of the activated subsystems." People had developed habits or cognitive structures that were based on sensorial pathways. "[The] subsystems would then fight according to their strengths for control of the final common path leading to action."[60]

Moreover, the early experimental psychologists (and the early behaviorists, for that matter) neglected the point of view of the experiencing person. They decided that "point of view" was not scientific. They did not pay attention to their subjects and especially neglected views of individuals whom they considered pathological. Therefore, they ignored data that came from dissociative experiences, including hypnosis. The psychologists were misled by their commitment to "scientific method." They would rather believe electrical responses than verbal reports, not realizing that so-called "objective behavior" can just as readily be faked as words.[61]

Those few psychologists who did use methods such as automatic writing and hypnosis to learn about personality found that projective tests such as the Rorschach Inkblot and the Thematic Apperception Tests gave better results. One such psychologist was Lillien J. Martin, an American who studied in Germany. She found that she got better results with tests designed to evoke spontaneous visual images than she did with automatic writing because the latter was hard to produce in subjects.[62]

No doubt, the exposure of many mediums as frauds also adversely affected the interest in dissociative phenomena and turned parapsychology into a disreputable pursuit for a scientist. In this regard, Flournoy's book, *From India to the Planet Mars,* was influential. Flournoy had refused to accept any supernatural explanations of Hélène Smith's revelations. His concept of cryptomnesia explained clairvoyance and telepathy. He also spelled out the various roles the medium's spiritist productions played in her life. They provided her with creative activity; they had a protective or defensive production (they warned her, comforted her, or helped to save her from blunders); they compensated for everyday frustrations by providing a vicarious, satisfying life; and they had a play function. Hélène Smith had not wanted to deceive, just play and fantasize; but in her case, as in many others, the fantasy life had gained control.

Flournoy's book was well received and was translated into English, Italian, and German. It became the basis for jokes, cartoons, and comedy skits, which shows its widespread impact. William James and Frederic Myers praised its scientific value.[63]

Janet also made it clear that he was very skeptical about parapsychology. Dessoir reported talking to him about it and commented: "His criticism contained an acid which would dissolve the platinum of facts."[64] Furthermore, by 1901, Frederic Myers, the leader of the Society for Psychical Research was dead, and later in the decade, one of his co-investigators, Frank Podmore, published two highly critical books on spiritualist phenomena. (See note 25.)

But the scorn of the scientific world for nontangible phenomena was rekindled by factors even more significant than rational explanations of mediumship. Of decisive importance were the death of Charcot in

1893, the subsequent exposure of the fraudulent behavior of some of his hysterical patients, and the attention given to the problems and pitfalls of hypnosis.

Upon his sudden death, Charcot was replaced at the Salpêtrière by men whose basic outlook was organicist. It was discovered that some of his followers had rehearsed dramatic hypnotic demonstrations with certain patients, which they then presented to Charcot as genuine. Charcot was accused of "unleashing a psychic epidemic."[65] A year after his death, the novelist, Léon Daudet (1867–1942), who had been a medical student on Charcot's ward, ridiculed him in a satiric novel, *The Death Peddlers*.[66] One of Charcot's favorite disciples, Babinski, re-belled against his teacher's concept of hysteria. Babinski said hysteria was nothing but the result of suggestion and could be cured by "persua-sion." In the years after Charcot's death, it was known that a visitor to the Salpêtrière, for a small fee, could entice one of the master's former patients to have an attack of *grande hystérie*.[67] Janet himself shared in the opprobrium that befell Charcot since he was identified as one of Charcot's ex-students. After 1893 Janet was the only physician at the Salpêtrière who persisted in utilizing hypnosis and who insisted hys-teria was not just a fake. The diagnosis of hysteria gradually disap-peared from French hospitals.[68]

Bernheim's reputation also suffered. About 1900, Bernheim was considered by many to be Europe's foremost psychotherapist. Ten years later, Bernheim was almost forgotten, replaced by newer men such as Dubois, who was considered more modern. In 1919, Bernheim died; Liébeault had already been dead for 15 years.

By the time of World War I, there was also a wave of reaction against the concept of multiple personality. Was an alternate personality "real" or the creation of the hypnotist? It was alleged that investigators had been tricked by patients and that psychotherapists had unknowingly elicited the phenomena they observed.[69] Moreover, hypnotists' extrava-gant claims raised suspicion. For example, a Colonel de Rochas touted his ability to regress his subjects to their infancy, birth, and fetal period and then to their previous lives. He also said his subjects could progress forward in time, and experience what was going to happen to them.[70]

But even conscientious hypnotists discovered there were drawbacks to hypnosis. Not everyone could become a good hypnotist. (Freud found this out.) Not everyone could be hypnotized. Many patients pretended to be hypnotized when they were not. Moritz Benedikt (1835–1920), the Viennese neurologist, Charcot, and Forel all had had this experience. It was discovered that hypnotized subjects respond with extreme sensitivity to the unconscious wishes of the hypnotist in order to please him. The hypnotist himself is often conditioned to do things in a certain way by his very first patient's responses. Thereafter, he develops certain expectations of results based on this initial experience. It was realized that the relationship between hypnotist and subject was highly reciprocal. These reports accumulated in the literature, and a powerful scientific reaction against the use of hypnosis took place.[71]

While Janet never turned against hypnotism, his work became suspect.[72] His reputation also suffered in several ways. He was attacked by the Nancy School because he preferred hypnotism to suggestion in the waking state. He said the two phenomena were distinct; they said they were related. He was severely reproached by the Catholic Church and called an atheist for his book *From Anguish to Ecstasy* where he discussed his observations and treatment of a woman, Madeleine, who had signs of the stigmata.[73] His claims for priority of certain discoveries were attacked by psychoanalysts. Moreover, in his later years he pursued other psychological interests and turned away increasingly from the fields of his original work. Before the war he became involved in creating a theoretical psychological synthesis of how the mind was organized. After World War I, he turned to the psychology of religion.

Perhaps personality factors played a role in Janet's eclipse. Janet was by nature a loner; he worshiped no master and founded no school. Perhaps the latter was because he never had a teaching post at the Sorbonne, nor did he have his own ward at the Salpêtrière. He taught at the Collège de France, an institution independent of the university and frequented mainly by specialists, foreign visitors, and the educated public. In an age that stressed the significance of emotions, he gave strangely little credence to them, and this in spite of the many troubled patients he treated. He wrote that he found it difficult to remember his dreams. He thought that falling in love is a kind of illness that would not happen if a person were perfectly healthy or balanced. Janet considered emotions a somewhat troublesome disturber of action.[74]

Oddly enough for a man of his experience, he believed that many patients were acting and playing, particularly as regards sexual deviations. He early expressed doubts about the truthfulness of many severe psychotics, eventually writing: "Most frequently, psychotics are acting. Don't believe one-fourth of what they say."[75]

As dissociation waned, psychoanalysis waxed.[76] Was this merely a temporal connection, or were there some causal factors? I think the latter, but the subject remains open for discussion. Psychoanalysis offered the concept of repression to replace the two dissociative concepts of amnesia and the hypnoid state.[77] Psychoanalysis abandoned hypnosis in favor of psychotherapy in the waking state. Moreover, psychoanalysis viewed the hypnotic state as regressive rather than as bringing forth a possibly healthier state.

There were still other differences. In designating dreams as wish-fulfillments, Freud turned dreams into less of a dissociative experience. Freud found the roots of creativity in regression rather than seeing creativity as indicative of some superior function. Freud emphasized the unitary personality. The stress was on personality integration as a goal in treatment. The later development in psychoanalysis of "ego psychology" is connected to this. Finally, people with psychotic conditions, which sometimes include dissociative displays, were regarded by Freud as unamenable to psychoanalytic treatment. Freud theorized that the emotional investment of a psychotic individual in another person is so limited, that no transference can be formed with the analyst.

For a few decades after World War I there was comparatively little scientific concern with hypnosis and multiple personality. Yet certain trends persisted. I find in Emile Coué's (1857–1926) system of auto-suggestion, popular in the twenties, echos of the influence of dissociation.[78] Otto Rank's *The Double* shows that there remained even within psychoanalysis an interest in dual personality.[79] Dual consciousnesses, perceived as "complementary" by William James, had a most surprising influence on modern physics. Niels Bohr, after reading this in James' work sometime between 1905 and 1912, said it prompted him to develop the theory of complementarity.[80]

Just as nineteenth-century disillusionment with materialistic approaches had the effect of turning attention to nonmaterialist subjects, so, early in the twentieth century did disappointment with parapsychology and hypnosis cause renewed emphasis on organic factors. Even psychoanalysis—although based on a nontangible "unconscious" and on verbal communication—relied on a theory of biological instincts.

The biological basis of psychoanalysis was rarely challenged until the 1940s.

Interest in multiple personality and hypnotism began to revive in the 1950s. In some Western countries, this was owing to a psychological awareness that psychoanalysis had helped foster. Concern with multiple personality and hypnosis has persisted up to the present, in spite of decreased interest in psychoanalysis and increased emphasis on pharmacology as the preferred scientific approach to problems of mental illness. Does this duality betoken at long last a new scientific sophistication, the first step toward the breakdown of the artificial distinction between body and mind? Or is it the newest chapter in the traditional materialist/nonmaterialist dichotomy?

Currently, the subject of multiple personality arouses wide interest, in connection with concerns about child abuse. Yet clinically and in legal circles, there continues to be much questioning of the use of hypnosis and the validity of the diagnosis of multiple personality. I think this ambivalence is evidence of the fact that scientific understanding is still artificially divided into categories of the organic and the nonorganic. But I do not want to end on a negative note. Perhaps modern studies of dissociative phenomena will finally lead scientists to a broad, authentic awareness of the inextricable linkage of the physical and mental worlds.

Notes

1. "Sur les divers états nerveux déterminés par l'hypnotisation chez les hystériques," *Comptes-Rendus Hebdomadaires des Séances de L'Academie des Sciences* 94 (1882): 403–405.
2. Pierre Janet, "Psychological Autobiography," in Carl Murchison, *A History of Psychology in Autobiography*, vol. I. Worcester: Clark University Press, 1930, p. 124.
3. Henri F. Ellenberger, *The Discovery of the Unconscious*. New York: Basic Books, 1970, p. 86.
4. Ronald W. Clark, *Freud, The Man and the Cause*. New York: Random House, 1980, p. 101.
5. "*Lucas 18, 14 verbessert.—Wer sich selbst erniedrigt, will erhöhet werden.*" Friedrich Nietzsche, *Menschliches, Allzumenschliches. Ein Buch für freie Geister*, in *Nietzsches Werke*, Part I, vol. II. Leipzig: C. G. Naumann, 1900, p. 91, N. 87.
6. Anna Balakian, "Symbolism," *The World Book Encyclopedia*, vol. 18. Chicago: Field Enterprises, 1975, p. 850.

7. Ellenberger, *Discovery,* p. 281.

8. Ibid., p. 166. Ellenberger provides a rich survey of late nineteenth-century fiction which was inspired by knowledge of hypnotism and multiple personality.

9. Marcel Prévost, *Le jardin secret.* Paris: A. Lemerre, 1904.

10. Arthur Schnitzler, *Leutnant Gustl.* Nachwort und Anmerkungen von Heinz Politzer. Berlin: S. Fischer, 1967.

11. Quoted in Jeremy Hawthorn, *Multiple Personality and the Disintegration of Literary Character.* New York: St. Martin's Press, 1983, p. ix.

12. Ernest R. Hilgard, *Divided Consciousness: Multiple Controls in Human Thought and Action.* New York: John Wiley, 1977, pp. 19, 22.

13. This statement of priority seems to have been first made by Ellenberger, *Discovery,* p. 127, and later authors have continued to accept his claim.

14. Emile Littré quoted in Ellenberger, *Discovery,* pp. 225–226.

15. Ellenberger, *Discovery,* p. 84.

16. William Crookes, "Notes of an Enquiry into Phenomena Called Spiritual, During the Years 1870–73," *Quarterly Journal of Science* (January 1874), in M. R. Barrington, ed., *Crookes and the Spirit World,* a collection of writings by R. G. Medhurst, general introduction by K. M. Goldney. New York: Taplinger, 1972, p. 113.

17. "Wallace, Alfred Russel," *Encyclopaedia Britannica,* vol. 23. Chicago: Encyclopaedia Britannica, 1951, p. 303.

18. Alfred Russel Wallace, *On Miracles and Modern Spiritualism. Three Essays.* London: James Burns, 1875, pp. vi–vii. A second edition appeared in 1896.

19. See, for example, *The New Revelation.* New York: George H. Doran, 1918 and *The Vital Message.* New York: George H. Doran, 1919. The "new revelation" was that of "spirit communication [which would follow]" a terrible war in different parts of the world (p. viii.) The proof of spirit communication lay in automatic writing. The "vital message" was that World War I was a religious event brought about by "the great Designer of all things" in order to purify and to reinforce Christianity "by the facts of spirit communion and the clear knowledge of what lies beyond the exit-door of death" (pp. 12–13).

20. Schopenhauer first published his ideas in 1819 in *The World as Will and Idea,* but the work began to receive attention only after 1850. It was widely quoted in the 1880s. Von Hartmann's *Philosophy of the Unconscious* appeared in 1869, a compilation of theories and evidence on the role of unconscious phenomena. It too was popular in the 1880s.

21. Ellenberger, *Discovery,* p. 313; Hilgard, *Divided Consciousness,* p. 153.

22. Ellenberger, *Discovery,* p. 314.

23. Frederic W. H. Myers, *Human Personality and Its Survival of Bodily Death,* with an introduction by Gardner Murphy, vols. I and II. New York: Arno Press, 1975. (Reprint of the edition published by Longmans, Green, 1903.)

24. "Myers, Frederic William Henry," *Encyclopaedia Britannica,* vol. 16, p. 42.
25. Frank Podmore, *Modern Spiritualism. A History and a Criticism,* 2 vols. London: Methuen, 1902; *From Mesmer to Christian Science. A Short History of Mental Healing.* New Hyde Park: University Books, 1963, originally published in 1909.
26. Hilgard, *Divided Consciousness,* p. 152. Hilgard took this anecdote from Alex Munthe, *The Story of San Michele.* New York: Dutton, 1929.
27. Théodore Flournoy, *From India to the Planet Mars. A Study of a Case of Somnambulism, with Glossolalia,* trans. Daniel B. Vermilye. New York: Harper and Brothers, 1900.
28. Ibid., pp. 9, 59, 441–442.
29. Ellenberger, *Discovery,* p. 316.
30. C. G. Jung, *Zur Psychologie und Pathologie sogenannter occulter Phänomene: Eine psychiatrische Studie.* Leipzig: Mutzel, 1902. An English translation appears in the *Collected Works,* vol. I. New York: Pantheon, 1957.
31. A history of hypnosis, called to my attention too late for me to draw on it for this chapter, is Dominique Barrucand's *Histoire de l'hypnose en France.* Paris: Presses Universitaires de France, 1967. I am grateful to Sherrill Mulhern for the reference.
32. Ellenberger discusses the case at length in *Discovery,* pp. 129–131.
33. E. Azam, "Double Consciousness," in D. Hack Tuke, ed., *A Dictionary of Psychological Medicine,* vol. I. London, J. & A. Churchill, 1892, pp. 401–406. A longer discussion of the case of Félida can be found in Azam's *Hypnotisme, double conscience et altération de la personnalité.* Paris: J. B. Baillière, 1887.
34. Charles Richet, "Du somnambulisme provoqué," *Journal de l'anatomie et de la physiologie normales et pathologiques de L'homme et des animaux* 2 (1875): 348–377.
35. Ellenberger, *Discovery,* p. 751.
36. August Forel, *Der Hypnotismus oder die Suggestion und der Psychotherapie,* 8th and 9th editions. Stuttgart: Ferdinand Enke, 1919. (The first edition appeared in 1889.)
37. Ellenberger, *Discovery,* pp. 95, 100.
38. Hilgard, *Divided Consciousness,* p. 129.
39. Alexander Bain, *The Emotions and the Will.* New York: D. Appleton, 1859. This has been reprinted as vol. V in series A of *Significant Contributions to the History of Psychology, 1750–1920.* Washington: University Publications of America, 1977; Charles Féré, *Sensation et mouvement. Études expérimentales de psychomécanique,* 2nd ed. Paris: Félix Alcan, 1900.
40. Ellenberger, *Discovery,* p. 290.
41. Gustav Le Bon, *Psychologie des foules.* Translated as *The Crowd: A Study of the Popular Mind.* New York: Macmillan, 1925.
42. Hippolyte Taine, *De l'Intelligence,* 2 vols., 4th ed. Paris: Hachette, 1883; Th. Ribot, *Diseases of Memory: An Essay in the Positive Psychology,* trans.

William Huntington Smith. New York: D. Appleton, 1882; and *The Diseases of Personality,* authorized translation, 4th, revised ed. Chicago: Open Court, 1906. These have been reprinted in vol. I, series C of *Significant Contributions to the History of Psychology, 1750–1920;* Gilbert Maire, *Bergson, mon maître.* Paris: Editions Bernard Grasset, 1935.

43. Ellenberger, *Discovery,* p. 168.
44. Flournoy, *From India,* p. 407.
45. C. G. Jung, "Cryptomnesia," *Collected Works,* vol. I. New York: Pantheon, 1957.
46. Max Dessoir, *Das Doppel-Ich.* Berlin: K. Siegismund, 1889. This first appeared as an essay in *Schriften der Gesellschaft für Experimental-Psychologie zu Berlin.* It was published separately in 1890, and a second edition appeared in 1896.
47. Ellenberger, convinced of Janet's originality and pioneering contributions to dynamic psychiatry, has attempted to raise his reputation from the backwaters where it had sunk in our century. Anyone writing on Janet must be grateful for Ellenberger's herculean research on this psychologist, which forms chapter 6 of *The Discovery of the Unconscious.*
48. Hilgard, *Divided Consciousness,* p. 29.
49. Pierre Janet, *L'Automatisme psychologique.* Paris: Félix Alcan, 1889.
50. Hilgard, *Divided Consciousness,* p. 5.
51. Ibid., p. 6.
52. Janet, *L'automatisme psychologique,* p. 318.
53. Janet, *The Mental State of Hystericals,* trans. by Caroline Rollin Carson. New York and London: G. P. Putnam, 1901. This has been reprinted as vol. II in series C of *Significant Contributions to the History of Psychology, 1750–1920.*
54. Quoted in Ellenberger, *Discovery,* p. 366.
55. Ellenberger, *Discovery,* p. 361.
56. Josef Breuer and Sigmund Freud, *Studies on Hysteria* (1893–1895), in *The Standard Edition of the Complete Psychological Works of Sigmund Freud,* ed. James Strachey. London: Hogarth Press, 1955, vol. II, pp. 12–13. Emphasis in original.
57. Ibid., p. 12.
58. The rivalry was aired publicly at two international meetings. The first was in 1907 in Amsterdam at the First International Congress for Psychiatry, Psychology, and the Assistance to the Insane. The second was in 1913 in London at the Seventeenth International Congress of Medicine. Janet delivered papers critical of psychoanalysis. Jung and Ernest Jones were present on both occasions. The nature of their participation is a matter of dispute. See Clark, *Freud,* pp. 241–242, 374; Ellenberger, *Discovery,* pp. 817–819; and Ernest Jones, *The Life and Work of Sigmund Freud,* vol. II, New York: Basic Books, 1955, p. 112.

Freud, who disliked public confrontations, attacked Janet in his autobiography, "An Autobiographical Study" (1925), in *Standard Edition,* vol. XX, 1959, pp. 30–31.

59. Hilgard, *Divided Consciousness,* pp. 116–216.

60. Ibid., p. 217.

61. I treat the subject of the psychologists' devotion to method in my book, *Freud in Germany: Revolution and Reaction in Science.* New York: International Universities Press, 1977, chapter 7.

62. Hilgard, *Divided Consciousness,* p. 138.

63. Ellenberger, *Discovery,* p. 782.

64. Quoted in ibid., p. 348.

65. Ellenberger, *Discovery,* p. 100.

66. Léon Daudet, *Les morticoles.* Paris: Charpentier, 1925. The novel begins with a line from Rabelais: "Science without conscience destroys the soul." Daudet continued to attack Charcot well into the twentieth century. See, for example, Daudet's *The Stupid XIXth Century,* trans. by Lewis Galantière. New York: Payson and Clarke, 1928, pp. 287–298.

67. Ellenberger, *Discovery,* p. 101.

68. Ibid., pp. 406, 377.

69. Ibid., p. 141.

70. Albert de Rochas, *Les vies successives. Documents pour l'étude de cette question.* Paris: Charconac, 1911.

71. Ellenberger, *Discovery,* pp. 171–173.

72. See Barrucand on Janet's "standing alone against the decline of hypnosis," *Histoire,* pp. 186–202.

73. Janet, *De l'angoisse à l'extase,* vol. I. Paris: Félix Alcan, 1926.

74. Ellenberger, *Discovery,* p. 401.

75. Quoted in ibid., p. 351.

76. For the view that psychoanalysis developed from the contemporary experience with dissociation, particularly with hypnotism, see Léon Chertok and Raymond de Saussure, *The Therapeutic Revolution: From Mesmer to Freud.* New York: Brunner/Mazel, 1979. Chertok and Saussure take the position that Freud's special contribution to studies of hypnotic phenomena and multiple personality was to call attention to the emotion ("the dynamic aspect") connected with these phenomena, a connection previous workers had ignored. See pp. 178–181.

77. Janet never gave up arguing against Freud's theory of repression. He reiterated the material in his attack on psychoanalysis at the 1913 London Congress of Medicine in the *Journal of Abnormal Psychology* (1915), in the *Journal de psychologie normale et pathologique* (1917), and in his book, *Les médications psychologiques* (1919). See chapter 11 of Janet, *Psychological Healing. A Historical and Clinical Study,* vol. I. New York: Macmillan, 1925. This has been reprinted as one of the volumes in E. T. Carlson, ed., *Classics in Psychiatry.* New York: Arno Press, 1976.

78. Emile Coué, *Self Mastery Through Conscious Autosuggestion,* Part One of

Better and Better Every Day. London: George Allen and Unwin, 1961. Coué was a chemist in Troyes, and after acquiring an interest in the healing powers of the mind, opened a free clinic in Nancy in 1910. *Self Mastery* was first translated into English in 1922, and Coué's autosuggestive method was enormously popular in the 1920s. Practioners intoned and reintoned the credo: "Every day in every way, I am getting better and better."

79. Otto Rank, *The Double. A Psychoanalytic Study*. Trans. and ed. with an introduction by Harry Tucker, Jr. Chapel Hill: The University of North Carolina Press, 1971. *The Double (Der Doppelgänger)* was first published as an article in 1914 (*Imago* 3: 97–164) and then as a book in 1925.

80. Quoted in Hilgard, *Divided Consciousness*, p. 200. Bohr referred to this passage in James' 1890 *Principles of Psychology*, vol. I: "*In certain persons . . . the total possible consciousness may be split into parts which coexist but mutually ignore each other,* and share the objects of knowledge between them. More remarkable still, they are *complementary*. Give an object to one of the consciousnesses, and by that fact you remove it from the other or others."

3. The Fragmenting of the Soul: Intellectual Prerequisites for Ideas of Dissociation in the United States

John C. Burnham, Ph.D.

At the beginning of the twentieth century, when the original, explicit concept of dissociation was at high tide, other distinctive concepts also appeared prominently in American intellectual and scientific discussions. The most significant concepts were those involved in attempts to demystify the soma as well as the psyche. Within the sciences of physiology, chemistry, and physics, wrote a New York scientist in 1914, "a complete explanation is to be found" for the phenomena of life.[1] This type of analysis, which led in the direction of materialistic explanation, provided not only contemporaneous intellectual context for ideas of dissociation but also evidence showing how and why those ideas evolved as they did.

It is not possible in the space of this chapter even to sketch the complete intellectual history over a century that would provide a full background for the growth of ideas of dissociation in the United States. Anyway, such a project would be superfluous, because we have Merle Curti's recent history of ideas about human nature in America, and it is just such ideas that are essential in understanding the history of dissociation. Curti shows how the rationalism of the Enlightenment gave way in the nineteenth century to more romantic ideas about humans and their emotions and irrationalities. Finally, Curti traces the development of scientific thinking about human nature in both the natural and social sciences. Like other intellectual historians, he places ideas of dissociation and the subconscious in a context of, first, romantic interest in affective experiences and, then, clinical/scientific interest in individuality and abnormality. Almost all of this thinking among American intellectuals had European roots, but the Americans, as Curti shows, often gave Old World ideas a stamp of their own and by the turn of the twentieth century were sending original findings back across the Atlantic.[2]

The special subject of dissociation, however, brings into focus the particular type of basic thinking about humans to which I have already referred, one usually known as reductionism. It was a type of thinking that was essential not only to ideas about dissociation but to concepts of all human thought and behavior as well as physiological processes. I therefore propose to argue in this chapter that the idea of dissociative phenomena is best understood as one of the mainstreams of nineteenth- and twentieth-century reductionism. Indeed, it can be contended that reductionism was the major intellectual strategy of the nineteenth and early twentieth centuries. Sometimes it was disguised as merely explanation, but when thinkers *explained* events, those thinkers almost always meant by "explaining" to account for the phenomenon in terms of events on a lower level, as people then understood it.[3] Reductionism was not just substituting regular natural laws for divine dispensations then, nor chemical and physical explanations for the vital or biological. Reductionism was a relentless pursuit of the idea that knowledge of components led to knowledge of causes. In this context, I propose to show how, in the psychological-medical realm, the initial concept was the soul, and the final intellectual product was dissociative phenomena.

This narrative is timely because from one point of view psychiatrists of the late twentieth century have reanimated the old phrenology debate: can a therapist treat just parts of a person or must that therapist treat the whole human being? Can treatment target functions which are localized, in one sense or another, or must the therapist, as in both behavioral and other psychotherapies, work with the entire organism? Moreover, finally, can the functioning of the whole organism be divided into meaningful fragments? But it was not just recently that these problems arose. The question of how to dissect a person's mind in order to understand him or her runs throughout both technical and more broadly cultural thinking about mental functioning and malfunctioning, from phrenology and neurophysiology to various psychological divisions and even whole multiple personalities. All were explanatory reductions.

In the nineteenth century, as I have already suggested, it was the soul that was being anatomized, either literally or figuratively. In the eighteenth and early nineteenth centuries, when well-educated Americans talked about the soul, they usually thought in very conventional terms, largely right out of Aristotle. They accepted the hierarchy of the vegetative, animal, and human souls. Then, in addition, they knew that the soul was coeval with life, or the life principle. (This aspect of the concept became the basis of vitalism, which functioned as the antithesis of one version of reductionism.) Finally, they often believed that the soul was the essence of the individual.[4]

As the nineteenth century wore on, many different thinkers struggled to maintain the idea of the soul. In a general way, the soul served to place man in the universe, and so comforting an idea therefore was not likely to be surrendered easily.[5] But in the United States two kinds of motives for trying to preserve belief in the soul stood out—the religious and moral, on the one hand, and, on the other hand, the psychological.

The religious and moral stake in the human soul was in turn twofold. First, the concept of the soul was necessary in any conventional idea of an afterlife. As George Bush, a New York University professor, explained in 1845, it was customary to "recognize the tripartite distinction of man's nature into *spirit, soul,* and *body*—that when the body is forsaken at death the *spiritual* and the *psychical* elements survive in coexistence together and constitute the *true man,* which in actual usage is commonly designated by the single term *soul*." Bush himself used both scripture and etymology to establish the closeness of psyche and spirit, and his focus was on what survived after the body was cut loose.[6]

The other aspect of the religious and moral belief in the soul was the fact that the concept of sin depended upon the idea that a single agent was necessary to carry the burden of guilt or innocence. However complicated a person might be, however numerous the constituents of his or her being, in the end he or she—the agent—either sinned or did not sin. Everyone, in those simpler times, understood that the soul was ultimately responsible for a person's actions. The soul was the essence of that person, that part of the person to which conscience and right reason spoke. Everyone knew that a person could not escape guilt simply by saying, "My hand did it," for the hand by itself had no soul but was merely subservient to the whole person's soul. "When I yield to my anger and speak a bitter word," wrote Lyman Abbott as late as

1885, "I am conscious that I have done wrong, not that some thing in me has done wrong, but that the whole I has sinned. . . . It is the soul that sins, not a faculty in the soul."[7] For conscientious folk, the soul was particularly important, then, because if there were no soul, there could be no sin. That is why I have been careful to speak of "the religious and moral" point of view, because even without religion, as in a secularizing society, the soul was still necessary to give meaning to the idea of right and wrong, for it served as the agent that decided to do right or wrong.

Psychological thinkers as well as religious writers therefore had a moral stake in maintaining the concept of the soul. But the psychological writers also had a technical interest in the concept. Insofar as they dealt with thinking, the soul was the agent that did the thinking. As a consequence, virtually any conventional psychological belief was based upon the idea of the soul.

Psychological writers could, in fact, cite empirical evidence of the existence of the soul. The evidence was consciousness, which, however interpreted—as perception, usually, or will—nevertheless provided a person with a sense of his or her unitary existence, the "I" or the "me" (philosophers were already arguing about the difference), but subjective awareness at any rate, even beyond "I think, therefore I am."[8]

One change did occur in this traditional and valuable concept. By the mid-nineteenth century, psychological writers tended to use the term "mind" in the place of "soul." A transitional English thinker of that period, George Moore, spelled out the common assumption about terminology: "To avoid confusion," he wrote, "the words soul, mind, and spirit will be employed as synonymous." What he was talking about was, in any case, as he put it, "that which is conscious of acting, thinking, and willing."[9]

Everyone knew that the unitary soul, or mind, operated through various divisions. Thomas Upham, professor of moral and mental philosophy at Bowdoin, expressed the general belief in 1840, although he still used soul and mind as functional synonyms:

It is undoubtedly true, that the human soul is to be regarded as constituting a nature which is one and indivisible; but still there is abundant reason for asserting that its nature can never be fully understood by contemplating it solely and exclusively under one aspect. There are, accordingly, three prominent and well-defined points of view in which the mind may be contemplated, viz., the Intellect, the Sensibilities, and the Will; otherwise expressed by the

phrases INTELLECTUAL, SENSITIVE OR SENTIENT, and VOLUN-
TARY states of mind.[10]

Regardless of the terminology, thinkers had traditionally established
various such categories of mental operations, which they, like Upham,
referred to as aspects of the mind or sometimes even divisions of the
mind. But even divisions of the mind would have no meaningful
context without the unifying soul.

The usual divisions through which the soul operated were the faculties. Like Upham, most thinkers followed the traditional divisions of
cognitive, appetitive, and volitional, or intellect, feelings, and will; and
most again tended to agree on at least the cognitive faculties: sensation,
perception, imagination, reflection, understanding, reason, and judgment. The appetitive and volitional faculties varied more according to
the different writers. But all of these divisions of the mind were still
only modes through which the soul operated. As Joseph Haven explained in 1857, "mental activity is, strictly speaking, one and indivisible. The mind is not a complex substance, composed of parts, but single
and one." He went on to say that the mind worked in many ways, and
upon different classes of objects. "The mind," he continued, therefore
"has as many distinct faculties, as it has distinct powers of action,
distinct functions, distinct modes and spheres of activity."[11]

Americans were largely old fashioned in their conceptualizations and
beliefs about the soul. In Europe, already in the eighteenth century, the
Romantics and pre-Romantics were beginning to secularize the concept
of the soul, not only into the mind, but into the self. The self indeed
turned out to be functionally the same as the soul, but now conceptualized upon secular considerations. And, eventually, this change in
ideas did penetrate even into American intellectual life.

Historians of ideas who have traced the concept of the modern self
note that a number of streams, including confessional and other Romantic literature and Kantian philosophy, came together in the mid-
and late eighteenth century, so that by the early nineteenth century the
notion of selfhood was available as a commonplace in Western thinking.
This self did have attributes and emphases: each self was distinctive and
original; no other one had developed in the same way. Moreover, the
new self was unique in time and belonged to a historical, not a static,
world. Finally, the self was separate and private, known fully only to

the one person. This separateness eventually led to an identity separate from society; in a more traditional society, the person and the society merged into one. By the mid-nineteenth century, distancing the self from society had given rise to still another term, individualism. At first, individualism had the negative connotation of antisocial and rebellious, and then later a positive connotation, especially in the United States, of the political and economic individualism that went along with political and economic liberty. The concept of individuality was resoundingly secular. By 1900, geologist Nathaniel Shaler could trace the process of universal individuation into every aspect of nature: "It is evident," he wrote, "that in Nature various impulses concur to establish more or less enduring assemblages of actions at certain points in the realm"; Shaler's general language of course reflects the fact that he did not distinguish the principle of individuality in molecules from that in humans. All were "enduring assemblages."[12]

Now it was true that even before the soul was converted into the self, Americans tended to emphasize separateness and individuality. In 1856, for example, clergyman Richard S. Storrs, Jr., explained that God "not only communicates life to the soul, and the highest life of which we can conceive, but he separates that life by a complete inward division, from every other. He creates the soul a self-conscious Person, by the motion of his [God's] will. He endows it with its separate faculties and being. He makes it, in every case, an individual agent. . . ."[13]

When, therefore, nineteenth-century Americans spoke of the individual self, they used the term interchangeably with the soul, which, too, was unitary and distinctive as well as private. Even secularizing the soul, then, did not suggest that it could be divided, not as self and not even when the term "mind" was used in a noncommittal way to refer to the soul—as in fact it was, continuously, in treatises on philosophical psychology.

The secularizing of terms was confusing in one area, literature. Traditionally one of the major concerns in modern Western writing was the internal struggle of evil, or the demonic, with the forces of right and decency in a person. This struggle was of course a struggle for possession of the soul, and the conflicting internal forces did not represent fragmentation in either European or American literature. When Whitman wrote, for example, "I am large, I contain multitudes," he still maintained the "I" that contained the multitudes. Only later was the convention of the fragmented self—or at least a radical refocusing on independent conflicting elements inside the person—conspicious in letters. And by that time, usually the twentieth century, reductionistic psychology was often a factor in authors' conceptualizations of a split or fragmented self, although as Masao Miyoshi points out, throughout the nineteenth century thinkers had more and more reason to feel torn asunder because they had to make choices—choices between belief and atheism, between political alternatives, between one way of life or another—and this pressure was particularly remarked on in the United States.[14]

In their more technical conceptualizations, educated Americans of the nineteenth century commonly employed two psychologies simultaneously or separately: Scottish commonsense moral philosophy, and association psychology. Both utilized the soul concept. In the Scottish school, moral sense communicated itself directly to the soul, which otherwise operated in a conventional way through faculties. And likewise the associationists, from John Locke on, assumed that there was a soul or self to entertain the ideas that they believed became associated.[15]

The first challenge to the unitary soul came, then, from a source quite outside traditional academic psychology and philosophy, namely, phrenology. Historians of medicine, psychology, and culture have all noted the large numbers of American thinkers who took up phrenology, or at least took it very seriously at some point. The evidence was quite plain. J. G. Spurzheim died in Boston in 1832 at the peak of an extraordinary public reception of his lectures there. George Combe made a remarkably successful tour of the United States from 1838 to 1840, drawing consistently large crowds of the best educated people. Even more significant, however, was the fact that for decades a whole new group of native professionals who called themselves phrenologists brought Gall's teachings to the generality of citizens everywhere, both educated and uneducated.[16]

Among leading thinkers, phrenology tended to die out by mid-century. One very important reason was that a number of articulate opponents attacked the phrenologists specifically because they divided the soul. Phrenological spokespersons denied that their ideas in any way impaired conventional religious beliefs; rather, these advocates asserted that the anatomical, on which phrenology was founded, could not impinge on the spiritual.[17]

It is true that phrenologists did use conventional psychological concepts, specifically the faculties and powers. They had, according to physician Charles Caldwell, delivered thinkers from Hume's skepticism about the mind by presenting, as Caldwell put it, "a rational and intelligible exposition of the mental powers, and . . . their relations to the moral, organic, and physical laws." But unfortunately Caldwell and others also talked about human propensities and even instincts that were rooted in particular "organs," or divisions, of the brain. Since the propensities were, everyone assumed, therefore inherited along with the physical constitution in which they were based, the phrenologists either wittingly or unwittingly involved in their ideas fatalism, or mechanistic determinism, as well as materialism. That moralistic Americans generally came to think that a person could cultivate and alter his or her phrenological propensities turned out to be of little moment for those interested in ideas and theory. The issue that phrenology raised was, if the brain was material and divided, the soul was in danger. Materialism and division were but two aspects of the same problem. With phrenology, wrote a critic of Caldwell, "The beautiful region of mental philosophy is to be converted into a barren *Golgotha,* or place of skulls. . . . The brain . . . is divided into several compartments, each of which exercises a separate function, producing a corresponding manifestation of the moral or intellectual faculties," by implication without the intervention of the soul. Another opponent of phrenology, writing in 1848, noted that if faulty behavior grew out of physical defects, the exact way in which the brain functioned was of little moment: "If Phrenology be true, the conduct of each individual is simply the result of a perpetual war among his organs; and the course of society the result of the conflicting organs of different heads! Let its principles prevail, and social and civil order disappear, and immorality in all its forms prevails."[18] To such critics, it made little difference if materialism opened the way to division of the soul or if fragmentation into organs led to materialism. The result was the same: denial of moral responsibility.

Even if phrenology in itself did not last, the pattern of thinking of people's behavior in terms of independent units based on brain divisions did persist, and it was central to reductionistic thinking about the mind or soul. As reductionism evolved in the nineteenth century, materialism and mechanism came to represent two independent lines of reductionists' strategies. Materialism proceeded particularly through neuroanatomy and neurophysiology, a line of inquiry that people at the time explicitly called the new phrenology because it involved another version of localizing brain function. An interest in speech, sometimes classified as a "faculty," provided the major initial impetus for the new studies using anatomy and physiology to destroy the idea of the unity of the mind. While the work of Broca and others is well known, it is worthwhile pointing out that one of the world pioneers of this exciting research that seemed to confirm brain sites for specific functions was the iconoclastic Cincinnati physician, Roberts Bartholow. Few Americans, even in science, were as dedicated as he was to materialistic reductionism, but they were well aware of materialistic ideas, both of the German philosophical variety and the more practical kind represented by Bartholow or the widely cited English psychiatrist, Henry Maudsley. Other devotees of neurology applied an equally enthusiastic naturalism to devise neurophysiological, reflex explanations for mysterious segmented behavior such as catalepsy, somnambulism, and even spiritualism.[19] But in truth neither philosophical nor practical materialism had a wide appeal in the United States. Instead, Americans tended to avoid the issue of materialism and to think rather in terms of mechanism.

Mechanism, however, was complex. Association psychology represented one common approach to mechanism, whether it was purely psychological or translated into a reflex equivalent of the association process (which presumably bypassed the soul). Oliver Wendell Holmes, for example, was well known for his interest in mechanism and fatalism. An even more pertinent example is another, younger Boston physician, Morton Prince, who in 1885 explicated a psychopathology based on association/reflex equivalents in which, as he wrote, "ideas, sensations, etc., are the ultimates, the final terms to which phenomena can be reduced." Prince went on to describe even Ego or self as but the aggregation of sensations associated together, and he concluded harshly, "There are no more grounds for the assumption of an autocratic Ego than there formerly [were] for assuming a spiritual entity for an explanation of mind." For Prince, a mix of motives in a person was sufficient to explain the (false) appearance of a single, willing unit, the soul or mind.[20] His dynamic outlook, of course, later made Prince a pioneer of dynamic psychiatry—and incidentally of dissociation.

A second approach to mechanism in Americans' thinking lay in the way in which they conceptualized the whole human organism, namely, as a machine. Now it is true that sometimes, as in popularizations and elementary school textbooks, the authors, to remove the mystery from life processes, compared human beings to steam engines. The most frequent comparisons of course depended on the fact that both children and locomotives burned fuel for energy. But as Charles Rosenberg has pointed out, nineteenth-century thinkers did not merely view humans as machines occasionally for explanatory purposes. Rather, the very language increasingly spawned mechanical metaphors for human activity, with the clear implication that human actions were understandable as mechanical events. In particular, writers, both popular and technical, employed physical and chemical language for the most mysterious part of human activity, nervous system functioning. As early as 1872, an American commentator was concluding, "Chemistry teaches that thought-force, like muscle-force, comes from food; and demonstrates that the force evolved by the brain, like that produced by the muscle, comes not from the disintegration of its own tissue, but is the converted energy of burning carbon. Can we longer doubt, then, that the brain, too, is a machine for the conversion of energy?"[21] By the late nineteenth century, in short, Americans more and more were conceptualizing the body as a fuel-consuming locomotive with limbs that moved like levers and pulleys, governed by a nervous system that worked like a telegraph or, later on, a telephone exchange system.

Now at this point it may appear that I have departed from my subject, namely, the intellectual background of the idea of dissociation; having brought it up, surely one ought to stick to the central topic of association psychology as such, upon which the notion of dissociation was based, rather than pursuing far afield only the mechanistic aspects of association. The explanation is, to begin with, that even today everyone knows at least some of the associationist beliefs that were so common 75 or 100 years ago, and to dwell upon them would be gratuitous. But more important, what gave dissociation its special significance was what happened in the realm of mechanism and reductionism. Let me therefore show that I am not digressing.

Most reductionism initially came out of nineteenth-century medicine. The drive of scientists to understand disease led directly to their emphasis on anatomy and structure. Physicians, in struggling to perfect both diagnosis and cure, sought the rational cause of the disease, and at first structural defect stood out.[22] When virtually everyone repeatedly spoke of the complex machinery of the human body, and anatomical pathology seemed so promising, it was no wonder that the medical reinforced the mechanical, and one important direction of development was to see human biology directly in terms of physics and chemistry, as symbolized, for example, in the turn-of-the-century work of Jacques Loeb.

But already in the late nineteenth century another type of thinking began to develop, one generally identified as the rise of physiology. In this type of thinking, reductionists came to utilize an intermediate unit, that is, a generalized physiological unit. These units came to be conceptualized as analogous to atoms existing in a moving but balanced system.

The first step in developing this new viewpoint was emphasizing the idea that the body was made up of protoplasm and divided into cells, each cell in turn comparable to an amoeba or other single-celled organism. Exactly how all of these cells worked together was not clear, but that each one had a function, no one doubted. Thus was born the new atomism, or what Frederick Kilgour has called atomicity and Garland Allen holistic materialism.[23]

Dynamic atomicity represented a major step beyond the older ideas of mechanism. Where, before, the ultimate purpose of the machine—typically the body—was to function automatically in overall terms of the environment or even the soul, in the new viewpoint each elemental unit came to have its own existence and own set of goals, creating within an entire system a dynamic equilibrium, such as Claude Bernard spoke of as the *milieu intérieur* and the American physiologist, Walter Cannon, in the twentieth century popularized as homeostasis.[24] The relationships between the various units in the atomistic system permitted investigators and popularizers alike to talk about meaningful actions and interactions within a set of relationships that could be virtually infinitely complex because of the number of units involved—a conceptualization of natural processes that permitted indefinite extension and was used for many decades thereafter.[25]

The "cell doctrine," as it was called in the nineteenth century, flourished in the Western world just when post-Daltonian chemistry was emphasizing the idea of atomistic thinking. From the beginning, as botanist Charles F. Cox shrewdly observed in 1890, the vitality of each cell in the body refuted the existence of a more general vital force such as was often identified with the soul. Moreover, the functioning of each cell had explanatory power even when the exact processes involved were as yet unknown. The authors of an 1899 school textbook, for example, concluded, "Thus we see that the health of our bodies depends on the nourishment and health of each separate cell. If we burn our hands, some of the cells are destroyed, and those lying near go to work to form new cellular tissue to take their place."[26]

By the end of the nineteenth century, the idea of the independence of the cell had developed substantially. The most spectacular extension was the germ theory of disease and the accompanying phagocyte theory, in which writers, now under the influence of Darwinism, pictured microscopic units locked in a miniature struggle for existence within the body.[27] By the twentieth century, other elements joined the cells, the germs, and the phagocytes in these internal dramas taking place in everyone's body. In 1916 physiologist J. J. R. MacLeod of Western Reserve, for example, after summarizing the extremely complex and sensitive interactions of physiological elements in the body, characterized the new outlook as one in which attention had shifted from simple physicochemical reductionism to a new reductionism, in which the constituent elements would be the interactions of what MacLeod called "normal" physiological events—the chemical and physical responses of reactive cells—or, as he put it, "the working and interdependence of the various functions which go to make up the normal." Such thinkers as MacLeod did not deny the importance of physics and chemistry, nor did they embrace any sort of vitalism. But they saw that available units, that is to say, units useful in reductionism, existed because there was in living organisms a complexity that could be resolved in terms of the very reactions carried out in the organism—each reaction with a direction or tendency and operating in a rapidly shifting environment. At the same time each reaction in turn constituted part of that environment. In effect, when investigators defined a function (or a "process" or "subsystem"), they had made an explanation.[28]

At first the elements in the new reductionism tended to be cellular, such as the gene, which came in the twentieth century to appear to determine so much of life. But soon particular complex chemicals joined the dynamic forces. By the 1890s bacteriologists were convinced that both chemical elements in the blood and phagocytes were involved in the defense against hostile microbes, and at about the same time other substances appeared on the scene, substances that could explain an enormous array of physiological events. The most conspicuous of these chemical units were the hormones and vitamins, each of which seemed to have a function, a target, and some regulatory mechanism based on other units.

Finally, as Robert E. Kohler, Jr., points out, when attention shifted in the early twentieth century from protoplasm to enzymes in the cells, a new term came into use, namely, biochemistry. Moreover, people sometimes spoke at first of "dynamic biochemistry," and even as the explicit word "dynamic" was dropped, the word "biochemistry" continued to carry the connotation of units in dynamic relationship with one another.[29]

The nervous system held a central place in this new dynamic atomicity, both because of the supposed integrative functions of nervous system elements and the continued fascination with biological determinism of human events. With the rise of the neurone theory in the 1890s, each nerve cell came to have an independent existence, with a significance greater than just any cell because it might make a much more significant, or possibly original, contribution to the whole system. Soon reflexes were recognized as physiological units, and, of course, then, conditioned reflexes. It was not enough, complained a biochemist in 1928, for him to be a chemical, a mechanical, and, finally, an electrical engineer; he would ultimately also have to be a psychologist to make a full explanation of life processes. So far had functional units developed by that time. Indeed, when in 1912 psychologist Shepherd Ivory Franz wrote explicitly about the "new phrenology" of brain localization, he criticized localizers not only because they were not clear about what localization meant but also because "mental processes" and "mental states"—the new units of the twentieth century—were just not mechanical enough to be localized.[30]

Around the turn of the twentieth century, then, thinkers who talked about dissociation had not only conventional mechanistic association theory on which to draw but a pattern of thinking in which the functional units of the human machine each had an independent existence and purpose of their own; the implied anthropomorphism in this description is true to the language thinkers used, as, for example, transparently, in the term multiple personality. Moreover, neither function nor purpose was under the control of the organism, whether animal, or man with a soul. Nor was the organism—or human—aware except derivatively of the battles of the germ and white blood cell or the urgent messages of the hormones. When, then, psychological elements became dissociated, they took on significance because, commonly, well informed and technically trained people already tended to think in terms of a dynamic atomicity. Indeed, the connection between medical background and interest in dynamic psychological thinking in the United States has been remarked on frequently. Perhaps on another occasion I can point out further in concrete detail how in fact physicians and scientists who among their peers were distinctive for their interest in dynamic psychiatry or psychology, had earlier taken a remarkable and conspicuous interest in the the germ theory of disease and in chemical determinants. For the time being I shall simply mention Stephen Y. Wilkerson's recent vivid case history of James J. Putnam of Boston.[31]

To underline the connection between dynamic atomicity and dissociation, let me cite one particularly homely example, namely, Worcester, McComb, and Coriat's famous 1908 book, *Religion and Medicine*. To illustrate dissociation, they used an independent group of memories such as would constitute a posthypnotic suggestion. And when they wished to account for the effects of certain associative phenomena (at that time frequently characterized after Bernheim as "suggestion"), the three authors appealed to physiological knowledge. In the case of "somatic changes" and dissociation in hysteria, they observed that:

It is obvious that effects of this character point to a psychic cause. . . . It is equally evident that this mind functions otherwise than our ordinary waking consciousness, for not only are its activities unattended by a sense of effort and conscious attention which characterizes the latter, but it operates in a field whither consciousness cannot follow it, attaining its results through the instrumentality of the sympathetic nervous system, the unstriped muscles, vasomotors, glands, etc., which lie outside the sphere of consciousness and over which conscious volition has no control. Moreover, it is to be remembered that these phenomena take place not as the result of mechanical nerve stimulation, but by suggestion.[32]

This suggestion, of course, operated through association.

One ultimate product of this kind of thinking was the "complex"—a dissociated group of memories that influenced thinking and behavior in a very distinctive way because of the emotion tied to them. Another was, naturally, as I have suggested, the multiple personality, in which a whole personality, again, with its own purposes, influenced the person. (And I shall not here explore the striking parallel of belief in individualism with belief in the individual existence of functional units in physiology and psychology.)

Finally, the great interest in instincts in the early twentieth century provided still another obvious version of this same type of independent unit. Instinct theorists suggested that inside the organism were drives, each one aimed in some direction or another and opposed by other drives and still other physiological constraints. So the instinct psychologists, such as William McDougall, commanded audiences conditioned not by mechanical models but by patterns out of the new reductionism of dynamic atomicity.

By the twentieth century, the very idea of mind was no longer equivalent to the notion of some sort of unity in a person—much less the spirituality of a soul. "Mind" had ceased to be a surrogate for a unified and responsible person. In psychologist James R. Angell's textbook of psychology, for example, a relatively conservative document, Angell explicitly disclaimed the soul, because it implied, he said, "something above and beyond the thoughts and feelings." But Angell went on also to disclaim similarly "the science of mind," because "the word *mind* ordinarily implies a certain continuity, unity, and personality, which is, indeed, characteristic of normal human beings; but which may, for all we can see, be wholly lacking in certain unusual psychical experiences. . . ."[33] Secularization, in short, did not save the soul, and, as I have already suggested, the more adventurous thinkers who worked with ideas of dissociation went much further than Angell in disbelieving the unity of the mind.

Over several decades, ideas of dissociation evolved in both the technical and popular literature of American medicine and psychology, especially through interest in hypnosis and allied phenomena. It has not been my task here to trace the way in which this happened. Rather, my object has been to suggest briefly the context of ideas that permitted the concept of dissociation to rise and flourish. But let me cite just one turn-of-the-century technical work to illustrate the pertinence to dissociation of my account of the way that Americans came to utilize the idea of a fragmented soul or mind. The example is a 1904 book by Boris Sidis and Simon P. Goodhart, *Multiple Personality*. The two authors not only employed physical science models with "constituent elements" and the "freedom of the individual elements" but equated "dissociated systems" with "neurone systems." However constrained their dynamic scheme, dissociation was part and parcel of their whole way of viewing nature as well as mind, and they, like other well-informed Americans, thought in terms of dynamic atomicity.[34]

As I indicated at the beginning, I have not mentioned a number of other aspects of American thought that were involved in ideas about dissociation. None seems to me to compare in fundamental importance and relevance with the fragmenting of the soul. Let me note for illustrative purposes the heredity–environment controversies of the late nineteenth and early twentieth centuries.[35] These controversies were of substantial importance in shaping some of the details in various thinkers' ideas, but dissociationists could come down on either side of the nature–nurture debate. Sidis and Goodhart, for example, employed the traditional European notion from Charcot and Janet that physical, that is, nervous system, degeneration was a precondition for dissociation to occur. Others came to believe that environmental occurrences—akin to hypnotism—sufficed to initiate the splitting off of psychological units. But in either case what dissociation most basically involved was the destruction of the unity of the person's thinking and willing.

The immediate successor to the first specific ideas of dissociation was, as I have already suggested, a widespread belief in determination of thought and action in which the determiners were not known to a person's consciousness. In the early twentieth century, American thinkers came to be thoroughly familiar with the idea of independent "hidden motives" in a person, motives that, like germs and phagocytes, were locked in mortal combat to determine what would happen in the organism. Of course, throughout the twentieth century, the idea of hidden motives had consequences for both intellectual and social developments about which historians are still writing.[36]

It remains to be observed that the traditional notion of the conscious, unitary, and even spiritual soul did not die out immediately. As late as 1908, for example, a writer in a popular magazine, Frank Marshall White, described New York psychiatrist Frederick Peterson's psychogalvanic version of the Jungian word association test as a "soul machine." Although the term "complex" appeared in the article, the writer never did employ the idea of dynamic, possibly conflicting psychological elements; in his view, the subconscious revealed by the machine was still an integral part of the person whom the "soul" represented.[37]

But such examples of the persistence of the traditional soul became increasingly unusual among educated Americans, not to mention scientists. The best evidence of how much had changed is the birth of personality theory in the 1930s, explicitly a reaction against the way that scientific psychologists had fragmented the person, a reaction against reductionism. Gordon Allport, the author of a classic pioneer work in the field, for instance, stressed the individuality of the person, but he ended up with a definition of personality that was right out of dynamic atomicity: "Personality is the dynamic organization within the individual of those psychophysical systems that determine his unique adjustments to his environment." Because of Allport's stress on the individual, indeed, the self, this unifying personality concept may have been a late model, secularized version of the early nineteenth century soul, but clearly the dynamic elements in it were a world away from traditional faculties.[38] It might be hard to see even the ghosts of phrenological propensities in the new definition, but the concept of independent elements of thought and impulse was clear indeed. How much, in turn, the 1930s' definition owed to specific ideas of dissociation, the product of the process of reductionism, I leave to my colleagues in this book to suggest, since it is outside the scope of this chapter.

In 1910, William James concluded that in philosophy and psychology, "Souls have worn out both themselves and their welcome, that is the plain truth."[39] His efforts in the face of that truth, like the efforts of others of his generation, involved attempting to salvage moral responsibility from the complex and mechanistic universe that reductionistic thinking had suggested. Analysis of that complexity into dissociated elements helped make sense of what might have appeared irrational in terms of the older psychology of the soul.

Notes

1. B. Horowitz, "The Ultra-Scientific School," *Popular Science Monthly* 85 (1914): 463.
2. Merle Curti, *Human Nature in American Thought: A History.* Madison: University of Wisconsin Press, 1980.

3. A recent discussion of the concept, in which analysis and complexity are distinguished, is Keith Stewart Thomson, "Reductionism and Other Isms in Biology," *American Scientist* 72 (1984): 388–390.

4. Perhaps the most cogent of the surveys of the concept are L. D. Arnett, *The Soul—A Study of Past and Present Beliefs*. Worcester, Mass.: Clark University, 1904; and H. B. Alexander, "The Conception of 'Soul,'" *Journal of Philosophy, Psychology and Scientific Methods* 9 (1912): 421–430.

5. See the philosophical context of this emphasis in Stephan Strasser, *The Soul in Metaphysical and Empirical Psychology*, trans. Henry J. Koren. Pittsburgh: Duquesne University, 1957, especially p. 9. One rather different Continental stream, vitalism, which was not central in American thought, is traced in Sergio Moravia, "The Capture of the Invisible. For a (Pre)history of Psychology in Eighteenth-Century France," *Journal of the History of the Behavioral Sciences* 9 (1983): 370–378.

6. George Bush, *The Soul; Or, An Inquiry into Scriptural Psychology, As Developed by the Use of the Terms, Soul, Spirit, Life, Etc., Viewed in Its Bearings in the Doctrines of the Resurrection*. New York: J. S. Redfield, 1845, p. 4.

7. Lyman Abbott, *A Study in Human Nature*. New York: Chautauqua Press, 1887 (1885), p. 15.

8. Standard reference works and histories of philosophical psychology detail the development of European ideas; American versions as they developed are described in Jay Wharton Fay, *American Psychology Before William James*. New Brunswick: Rutgers University Press, 1939.

9. George Moore, *The Power of the Soul Over the Body, Considered in Relation to Health and Morals*. New York: Harper & Brothers, 1847, p. 7.

10. Thomas C. Upham, *Elements of Mental Philosophy, Embracing the Two Departments of the Intellect and the Sensibilities*, 2 vols. New York: Harper & Brothers, 1840, I, p. 47.

11. Joseph Haven, *Mental Philosophy, Including the Intellect, Sensibilities, and Will*. Boston: Gould and Lincoln, 1859 (1857), p. 29. Fay, *American Psychology*, summarizes the literature lucidly.

12. See especially John O. Lyons, *The Invention of the Self: The Hinge of Consciousness in the Eighteenth Century*. Carbondale: Southern Illinois University Press, 1978. Also see Morse Peckham, *Beyond the Tragic Vision, The Quest for Identity in the Nineteenth Century*. New York: George Braziller, 1962; Koenraad W. Swart, "'Individualism' in the Mid-Nineteenth Century," *Journal of the History of Ideas* 23 (1962): 77–90; and Nathaniel Southgate Shaler, *The Individual, A Study of Life and Death*. New York: D. Appleton, 1901, p. 71.

13. Richard S. Storrs, Jr., *The Constitution of the Human Soul, Six Lectures Delivered at the Brooklyn Institute, Brooklyn, N.Y.* New York: Robert Carter, 1856, p. 35.

14. Particularly pertinent is the discussion of "decomposition" in Robert

Rogers, *A Psychoanalytic Study of the Double in Literature*. Detroit: Wayne State University Press, 1970, especially pp. 11–13. There is a substantial literature on the "double" in literature, most notoriously Dr. Jekyll and Mr. Hyde, and a cogent summary of this approach to dissociation in fiction is the editorial comment in Morris Beja, *Psychological Fiction*. Glenview, Ill.: Scott, Foresman, 1971, pp. 276–280. See also Masao Miyoshi, *The Divided Self, A Perspective on the Literature of the Victorians*. New York: New York University Press, 1969, especially p. xv. To Victorians in general, what Matthew Arnold called "the dialogue of the mind with itself" therefore took on increasing significance as doubt opened the way to making choices. Matthew Arnold, *The Poems of Matthew Arnold, 1840–1867*. London: Oxford University Press, 1926, p. 1; and, in general, Walter E. Houghton, *The Victorian Frame of Mind, 1830–1870*. New Haven: Yale University Press, 1957.

15. Fay, *American Psychology*. D. B. Klein, *The History of Scientific Psychology, Its Origin and Philosophical Backgrounds*. New York: Basic Books, 1970, pp. 394–396.

16. See especially John D. Davies, *Phrenology, Fad and Science, A 19th-Century American Crusade*. New Haven: Yale University Press, 1955; and Madeleine B. Stern, *Heads & Headlines, The Phrenological Fowlers*. Norman: University of Oklahoma Press, 1971.

17. See previous note and David de Giustino, *Conquest of Mind, Phrenology and Victorian Social Thought*. London: Croom Helm, 1975.

18. [Charles Caldwell], "Moral Aspects of Phrenology," *Christian Examiner* 17 (1834): 254; and N. L. Rice, *Phrenology Examined, and Shown to be Inconsistent with the Principles of Phisiology, Mental and Moral Science, and the Doctrines of Christianity, Also an Examination of the Claims of Mesmerism*. New York: Robert Carter, 1848, pp. 90–91, 142.

19. James P. Morgan, "The First Reported Case of Electrical Stimulation of the Human Brain," *Journal of the History of Medicine and Allied Sciences* 37 (1982): 51–64; E. F. Brush, "The Faculty of Speech," *Popular Science Monthly* 24 (1884): 793–794; Edward M. Brown, "Neurology and Spiritualism in the 1870's," *Bulletin of the History of Medicine* 57 (1983): 573–575. Basic background and distinctions are in Frederick Gregory, *Scientific Materialism in Nineteenth Century Germany*. Dordrecht: D. Reidel, 1977, especially pp. x–xi.

20. Oliver Wendell Holmes, *Mechanism in Thought and Morals, An Address Delivered Before the Phi Beta Kappa Society of Harvard University, June 29, 1870. With Notes and Afterthoughts*. Boston: J. R. Osgood, 1871; and Morton Prince, *The Nature of Mind and Human Automatism*. Philadelphia: Lippincott, 1885, especially pp. 102, 133–142.

21. Charles Rosenberg, *No Other Gods; On Science and American Social Thought*. Baltimore: Johns Hopkins University Press, 1976, p. 4; and T. H. Huxley et al., *Half-Hours with Modern Scientists, Lectures & Essays*. New Haven: C. C. Chatfield, 1872, pp. 60–61.

22. A modern perspective on these origins is George L. Engel, "The Need for a New Medical Model: A Challenge for Biomedicine," *Science* 196 (1977): 129–136.

23. Philip J. Pauly, "The Appearance of Academic Biology in Late Nineteenth-Century America," *Journal of the History of Biology* 17 (1984): 369–397. See, for example, Frances Emily White, "Protoplasm," *Popular Science Monthly* 21 (1882): 361–370; Frederick G. Kilgour, "Scientific Ideas of Atomicity in the Nineteenth Century," *Proceedings of the Tenth International Congress of the History of Science*, 2 vols. Paris: Hermann, 1964, I, 329–331; and Garland E. Allen, *Life Science in the Twentieth Century*. New York: John Wiley, 1975.

24. L. L. Langley, ed., *Homeostasis, Origins of the Concept*. Stroudsburg, Pa.: Dowden, Hutchinson & Ross, 1973.

25. See, for example, Ernest Borek, *The Atoms Within Us*. New York: Columbia University Press, 1961.

26. Charles F. Cox, *Protoplasm and Life, Two Biological Essays*. New York: N. D. C. Hodges, 1890, especially pp. 5, 29–37. C. H. May and Smith Ely Jelliffe, *May's Anatomy, Physiology, and Hygiene, For Use in Primary and Intermediate Schools*, 4th ed. New York: William Wood, 1899, p. 17.

27. See, for example, Andrew McClary, "Germs Are Everywhere: The Germ Threat as Seen in Magazine Articles 1890–1920," *Journal of American Culture* 3 (1980): 33–46.

28. J. J. R. MacLeod, "Vitalism and the New Physiology," *Journal of Laboratory and Clinical Medicine* 2 (1916): 209–212. It should no doubt be noted that ecological thinking was evolving in other areas of biology at this same time. Even more to the point was the rise of general biology at the turn of the century.

29. Robert E. Kohler, Jr., "The Enzyme Theory and the Origin of Biochemistry," *Isis* 64 (1973): 181–196.

30. Allen, *Life Science*. Albert P. Mathews, "The Chemistry of Life," *Science News-Letter* (May 5, 1928), p. 280. S. I. Franz, "New Phrenology," *Science* 35 (1912): 321–328.

31. Stephen Y. Wilkerson, "James Jackson Putnam and the Impact of Neurology in Psychotherapy in Late Nineteenth-Century America." Doctoral dissertation, Duke University, 1970. Nor are genetic or developmental assumptions discussed here.

32. Elwood Worcester, Samuel McComb, and Isador H. Coriat, *Religion and Medicine, The Moral Control of Nervous Disorders*. New York: Moffat, Yard, 1908, pp. 24–25, 86–87.

33. James Rowland Angell, *Psychology, An Introductory Study of the Structure and Function of Human Consciousness*, 4th ed. New York: Henry Holt, 1908, p. 2. Some of the flavor of the contemporary debate around the change can be found in such writings as James T. Bixby, "Is the Soul a Baseless Hypothesis?" *Bibliotheca Sacra* 47 (1890): 191–215.

34. Boris Sidis and Simon P. Goodhart, *Multiple Personality, An Experimental Investigation into the Nature of Human Individuality*. New York: D. Appleton, 1904, especially pp. 32, 356–360.

35. The standard work is of course Hamilton Cravens, *The Triumph of Evolution, American Scientists and the Heredity-Environment Controversy 1900–1941*. Philadelphia: University of Pennsylvania Press, 1978.

36. See, for example, John C. Burnham, "The New Psychology: From Narcissism to Social Control," in John Braeman, Robert Bremner, and David Brody, eds., *Change and Continuity in Twentieth-Century America: The 1920's*. Columbus: Ohio State University Press, 1968, pp. 351–398.

37. Frank Marshall White, "The Soul Machine," *Harper's Weekly* (December 19, 1908), pp. 12–13, 32. See, for example, G. T. W. Patrick, "The Search for the Soul in Contemporary Thought," *Popular Science Monthly* 78 (1911): 460–468.

38. Maurice Mandelbaum, *History, Man, & Reason, A Study in Nineteenth-Century Thought*. Baltimore: Johns Hopkins University Press, 1971, pp. 365, 367; Gordon W. Allport, *Personality, A Psychological Interpretation*. New York: Henry Holt, 1937, especially p. 48; and John C. Burnham, "Historical Background for the Study of Personality," in Edgar F. Borgatta and William W. Lambert, eds., *Handbook of Personality Theory and Research*. Chicago: Rand McNally, 1968, especially p. 73.

39. William James, *A Pluralistic Universe: Hibbert Lectures at Manchester College on the Present Situation in Philosophy*. London: Longmans, 1909, p. 210.

4. Explanations of Dissociation in the First Half of the Twentieth Century

Adam Crabtree

There were a number of important developments in the investigation of dissociative phenomena in the first half of the twentieth century. There were, for instance, the new directions taken in the study of hypnosis when Clark Hull introduced that field to the statistical method of experimental research. There were also advances in the study of automatisms, such as automatic writing and crystal gazing, undertaken by both psychologists, like Anita Muhl and Morton Prince, and psychical researchers of the British Society for Psychical Research. And, of course, a number of intriguing cases of multiple personality occur during this period. Not the least of them was the Doris Fischer case—the most extensively documented case in history—which initiated a quaint byway of inquiry into the relationship of multiple personality to possession. However, I would like to limit the scope of this chapter to looking at a few of the main attempts made during the first half of this century to fathom the basic nature of dissociation.

To begin a discussion of theoretical concepts of dissociation as they developed in the early 1900s, I must first step back a little in time. The dawn of the twentieth century found a great deal of excitement in psychological circles about the recently identified issue of dissociation and its related phenomena. It had been only 14 years since Pierre Janet had raised that topic and used that term in his three great articles in the *Revue Philosophique*.[1] In those articles and in his *L'Automatisme psychologique,*[2] published two years later in 1889, Janet touched upon virtually all of the areas identified by Dr. Carlson in chapter 1, and attempted to unify them within the framework of the "subconscious."[3] From that time on it would be virtually impossible to discuss the subject of dissociation without referring to the work of that remarkable Frenchman.

Although Janet's formulation of dissociation and the subconscious was the common starting point for many to take up their own researches, certain divergences in understanding these issues soon became apparent. From the beginning, Janet claimed that he was simply describing some remarkable phenomena he had come across in working with the disturbed, particularly hysterics, and insisted he was not drawing any broader theoretical conclusions about the nature of human personality. But it was inevitable that those who followed would not leave such questions alone. So it was that by 1907 Janet could write, with some apparent bewilderment: "You ask me to take a stand with regard to the metaphysical theories which are developing today and which seem to have for their point of departure the study of phenomena formerly described by me under the name of the "Subconscious." These studies, already old, since I published them between the years 1886 and 1889, do not permit me to take part in this serious quarrel; they have a much more restricted and much less ambitious range. While the researches of the present day, whether they have a spiritualistic or a materialistic tendency, attain to the summit of the highest metaphysics, my old studies, very modest as they were, simply endeavored to throw light upon, describe and classify certain phenomena of pathological psychology."[4]

This quotation is taken from Janet's contribution to "A Symposium on the Subconscious" which was made up of articles by a number of authors and appeared in several issues of the *Journal of Abnormal Psychology* in 1907. Since that "Symposium" brought into focus most of the principal theoretical issues of dissociation as pondered in the first part of the twentieth century, I would like to use it as a starting point for a discussion of the thinking of the main researchers of that period.

Morton Prince was editor of the *Journal of Abnormal Psychology* and also one of the chief speculators on the nature of dissociation and the subconscious. At the beginning of the "Symposium" he contributed a Prefatory Note in which he identified six meanings which had been attached to the term subconscious. This is very helpful for our purposes, for they summarize the principal ways in which the problem of explaining dissociation was approached at that time.

The first meaning of subconscious was its use to describe that portion of our field of consciousness which is outside the focus of attention at any given moment; it designated the marginal states at the fringe of consciousness. This is the meaning with least relevance to our discussion.

The second meaning well describes Janet's formulation and is worth quoting in full:

Subconscious ideas are dissociated or split-off ideas; split off from the main personal consciousness, from the focus of attention—if that term be preferred—in such fashion that the subject is entirely unaware of them, though they are not inert but active. These split-off ideas may be limited to isolated sensations, like the lost tactile sensations of anesthesia; or may be aggregated into groups or systems. In other words, they form a consciousness coexisting with the primary consciousness and thereby a doubling of consciousness results. The split-off consciousness may display extraordinary activity. The primary personal consciousness as a general rule is of course the main and larger consciousness; but under exceptional conditions, as in some types of automatic writing, the personal consciousness may be reduced to rudimentary proportions, while the secondary consciousness may rob the former of the greater part of its faculties and become the dominant consciousness.[5]

This formulation, an excellent capsulization of Janet's view, is the touchstone against which all other formulations universally have been measured.

In the third meaning, subconscious states become personified and are spoken of as the "subconscious *self*," the "hidden *self*," and so forth. This usage moves away from the mere study of the abnormal and holds that a subconscious self is a part of the mind of *every* human being. Thus, *every* mind is double; we all possess two selves, with the subconscious self having powerful effects upon the feelings, thoughts, and reactions of the conscious self.

The fourth meaning simply extends the third to include not only those ideas which remain active below the surface of awareness, but also those which are inactive—forgotten or out of mind.

The fifth meaning is basically that of Frederic Myers, who takes the concept of the subconscious self into the realm of metaphysics with his notion of the "subliminal self."

The sixth meaning interprets the phenomena that are usually considered to be the activity of dissociated ideas in purely physiological terms. This is a revised form of William Carpenter's old notion of "unconscious cerebration"[6] in which subconscious phenomena are explained as pure neural processes unaccompanied by any mental activity.

These are the six meanings of the term "subconscious" which Prince was able to identify as current in 1907. Within these six meanings are embedded some serious differences of opinion about the nature of dissociation and how it occurs. These conflicting opinions can be reduced to three theoretical issues: (1) the physiological versus the psychological explanation of dissociation; (2) dissociation and the second self; and (3) the Freudian view of dissociation. I would like to take up these three issues now to give you an idea of the explicit thinking about dissociation during the first decades of this century.

The Physiological versus the Psychological Explanation

The first issue—physiology versus psychology—was debated by Hugo Münsterberg and Morton Prince in the pages of the *Journal of Abnormal Psychology*. Münsterberg, professor of psychology at Harvard, championed the physiological interpretation of the subconscious as given in the sixth meaning mentioned earlier. In the "Symposium,"[7] Münsterberg takes exception to any notion of the subconscious implying that mental operations take place outside our conscious awareness. He points out that all explanations of that type see the subconscious as having two aspects. The first is that it is a reservoir for subconscious ideas. The second is that it is a mental workshop which manufactures the products of thought, insofar as they are not elaborated consciously—this notion being needed to explain the "evidently synthetic labor which goes on independently of our conscious control."

To disprove the view that mental operations can happen outside our conscious awareness, Münsterberg first of all insists that there is no scientific justification for presuming the existence of subconscious memories. He believes that this idea derived from abnormal psychology (particularly Janet's experiments), and that a close look at the facts would show that they can be adequately explained by the theory of normal remembering, which holds that a memory is revived simply as the result of a stimulation of the brain. There is no need, he says, to talk about any *psychical* traces of memories.

With regard to the "mental workshop" aspect of the subconscious, Münsterberg points out that the various functions of the body carry on very well in doing their tasks without any mental intervention to direct them. Why, then, cannot the central nervous system also produce physiological processes that lead to well-adjusted results—that is, to apparently purposive sensorial excitements and motor impulses? Münsterberg concludes by stating his own theory:

The dissociated idea is psychologically not existent just as the ticking of the clock in my room does not exist for me when my attention is turned to my reading; the ticking reaches my brain and may there have after-effects, but the sound-sensation is inhibited. In this way all that which suggested the theory of the mental subconscious becomes simply increased or decreased inhibition.[8]

Morton Prince, who was both editor of the *Journal of Abnormal Psychology* and professor of neurology at Tufts Medical School at that time, strongly disagreed with Münsterberg and decided to use his contribution to the "Symposium"[9] as an opportunity to take him to task. In doing so Prince reiterated his own view of dissociation which was, in fact, one of the chief contributions to theory about that subject after Janet, giving the definitive formulation of certain key issues implicit in Janet's system.

Prince puts the debated questions this way: "Do phenomena which appear to be the manifestations of a subconscious intelligence necessitate the posulation of dissociated ideas, or are these phenomena compatible with the interpretation that they are due to pure physiological processes without psychical correlates?"[10]

Prince provides a preliminary answer in these terms:

The only grounds I have for believing that my fellow beings have thoughts like myself are that their actions are like my own, exhibit intelligence like my own, and when I ask them they tell me they have consciousness, which as described is like my own. Now, when I observe the so-called automatic actions, I find that they are of a similar character, and when I ask of whatever it is that performs these actions, Whether it is conscious or not? the written or spoken reply is, that it is and that consciously it feels, thinks and wills the actions, etc. The evidence being the same in the one case as in the other, the presumption is that the automatic intelligence is as conscious as the personal intelligence. The alternative interpretation is, not that a physiological process is lying, because lying connotes ideas, but that in some way it is able to rearrange itself and react to another person's ideas expressed through spoken language exactly in the same way that a conscious intelligence lies.[11]

To deal with the issue Prince uses the phenomenon of automatic writing as the testing ground. Automatic writing is produced when an individual, pencil in hand, writes out messages which his or her ordinary conscious mind has no part in producing. The ordinary conscious mind—let us call it intelligence no. 1—may be completely alert, carrying out some engrossing task unrelated to the writing that is taking place. Or it may be in a clouded or nearly extinguished state while the writing happens. In the writing itself there appears another intelligence—let us call it intelligence no. 2. This intelligence communicates without the participation of intelligence no. 1, although in some cases intelligence no. 1 is fully aware of the communication as it occurs.

Prince points out that the evidence of automatic writing is difficult to reconcile with a physiological interpretation of dissociation phenomena. For the writings often do not consist merely of words, phrases, or paragraphs which are memories of previous experiences. Rather they are frequently elaborate compositions of great complexity and originality. Moreover, the products of automatic writing manifest themselves as the creation of a personality quite unknown to the main personality of the writer, but having all the characteristics we ascribe to individual human personality. The question then is, how a nonpersonal, purely physiological process could manufacture such an elaborate and original creation?

Prince is ready to agree that physiological cerebration and psychical ideas may well be inseparable events. The only question is "whether physiological cerebration is accompanied by, belongs to, or *is* another aspect of ideas." Considering the nature of the facts that must be explained, the physiological process of itself cannot, he insists, be seen as the *originator* of the ideas.

In his rather extensive psychological writings,[12] Prince offers an alternative framework for understanding dissociation. It is based on a clarification and a careful definition of terms which up to then had been employed in various contradictory ways. He points out that "subconscious" and "unconscious" have often been used as synonyms, but in a confusing way because they are applied to two or three different classes of facts. He undertakes to replace the term "subconscious" as derived from Janet with the term "coconscious" and to reserve the term unconscious to those basically physiological processes that are devoid of the attributes of consciousness.

Thus unconscious refers to those processes having to do with the registration, storage, and retrieval of memories that happens on a purely neurological level. But coconscious ideas or coconsciousness has to do with a dissociated consciousness or consciousnesses that coexist with one's normal personal consciousness. Prince points out that coconscious ideas have been called unconscious (for example, by Freud) because the personal consciousness is not aware of them. But this designation is confusing and so should be avoided.

Coconscious ideas include states we are not aware of because they are not the focus of our attention, and also pathologically split-off and independently active ideas or systems of ideas, such as occur in hysteria and reach their most striking form in coconscious personalities and automatic writing.

Prince prefers the term coconscious to Janet's subconscious for two reasons. First, because it expresses the simultaneous coactivity of a second consciousness. And second, because the coactive ideas or idea systems may not be outside the awareness of the personal consciousness at all. They may be recognized by the personal consciousness as a distinct consciousness existing alongside it.

Thus, through his redefinition of terms, Prince makes simultaneous activity of two or more systems of consciousness in one individual the key element in dissociation. He thereby moves the issue of amnesia or lack of awareness by one system of another into the background, making it a secondary, nonessential element. Prince was one of the few to provide a theoretical framework for dissociation in which any combination of interawareness among the coconscious systems was possible.

Prince's view of coconsciousness and dissociation provides him with a ready explanation for hysteria and multiple personality. Prince includes under the category of hysteria a broad range of disturbances from a localized anesthesia to certain of the insanities. He says that hysterics manifest two kinds of symptoms, physical and mental. The physical may include anesthesias, paralysis, vomiting, pains, convulsions, and so forth. The mental include irritability, change of moods, abnormal instability and suggestibility, and fixed ideas—especially phobias. Prince points out that mental symptoms may be manifest without any accompanying physical symptoms and that they often constitute a true alteration of the personality. But whether the symptoms are mainly physical or mental, they are to be considered the manifestation of dissociated ideas or systems of ideas which have co-conscious existence alongside the normal consciousness of the individual and which intrude into his or her waking life through the symptoms.

For Prince, multiple personality is simply a more complete elaboration of the hysterical condition, now with the dissociated symptom-complex forming one or more phases of the multiple individual. His view is summed up in this quotation:

Multiple personality, of course, is the same thing as dissociated or what is also termed disintegrated personality, where the normal individual alternately becomes disintegrated and healthy, changing back and forth from disease to health; or, from the point of view of this study, becomes alternately a hysteric and healthy. Where there are more than two personalities, we may have two hysteric states successively changing with each other and, it may be, with the complete healthy person.[13]

While this view of multiple personality provides a neat theoretical framework, pinpointing that condition as the extreme end of a continuum of dissociation, Prince's particular understanding of it provides serious practical problems. For if multiple personality is simply the alteration between hysterical personalities and the healthy person, then the physician's obvious task is to identify that one healthy personality in order to strengthen it and get rid of the others. In other words, he has to make a godlike judgment about which inner systems in his client are worthy of salvation and which are not. This was Prince's dilemma with his famous "Miss Beauchamp" case, described in some detail in *The Dissociation of a Personality* which Prince published in 1905.[14] One watches with some suspense as, by his own account of the case, he fastens now on one personality, now on another to be the lucky survivor—the "real" Miss Beauchamp—while at the same he attempts to squeeze out the one personality who was never a serious candidate for that position, the liveliest and most interesting of the bunch—the Sally personality.

Nevertheless, with his formulation of the dissociation continuum and his detailed analysis of multiple personality in terms of it, and especially with his notion of coconsciousness—a notion that sidesteps the ambiguity of the term unconscious and emphasizes the coactivity of dissociated systems—Prince made a significant contribution to the advancement of the theory of dissociation.

Dissociation and the Second Self

Let us now move on to the second of the theoretical issues connected with dissociation that was being bandied about in the first half of this century. Among those who were grappling with the issue of the subconscious were some who were bold enough to go beyond Janet's descriptive classification of the phenomenon and talk about the subconscious as a cohesive living entity in its own right. To the question, Is it proper to personify subconscious states to the extent that one would speak about a subconscious *self,* a hidden *self,* or a second *self*? they answered a definite yes. But although there were many who gave an affirmative response,[15] how they conceived that second self varied radically. I would like briefly to consider two researchers who affirmed the existence of a second, subconscious self in us all, but who came to very different conclusions about that self. They are Boris Sidis and Frederic Myers.

Boris Sidis. Boris Sidis was a student and later an associate of William James who went on to develop a psychology that bore his own special stamp. Sidis was one of those early researchers to feel at home in the laboratory, and in his psychological experiments tended to make a great deal of use of instrumentation. Nevertheless, his main area of inquiry was suggestion and its connection with hypnotic and hypnoidal states, a field which did not at that time lend itself to extensive measurement.

Sidis' experimentation with suggestibility in both normal and abnormal subjects led him to the conclusion that in everyone there coexist two streams of consciousness and that these constitute two selves: the waking self and the subwaking self. He first formulated his views on these two selves in an important work entitled *The Psychology of Suggestion* and elaborated on them in a number of later writings.[16]

For Sidis, the waking self is the ruling self, "a person having the power to investigate his own nature, to discover faults, to create ideals, to strive after them, to struggle for them, and by continuous, strenuous efforts of will to attain higher and higher states of personality."[17]

The subwaking self is a consciousness which has an awareness broader than that of the waking self. The submerged, subwaking self knows the life of the waking self, but the latter does not know the former.

The subwaking self has certain striking characteristics. It is first of all stupid, totally lacking in critical sense. It is also highly suggestible, and will follow all commands in an extremely literal way. Furthermore, the subwaking self is devoid of morality, apparently being willing to carry out any act, no matter how destructive, without scruple. Also, being both suggestible and amoral, the subwaking self is very susceptible to the emotional forces that operate in crowds and mobs. At bottom, then, the subwaking self lacks all personality and individuality; having no will and no goals, it is basically a "brutal self."

However, Sidis tells us that the subwaking or subconscious self can make some progress toward self-awareness and becoming a self-conscious personality. Indeed, it can become so individualized as to lead a submerged life perfectly independent of that of the waking self. It can, as a matter of fact, rise to the surface and assume control of the organism. For instance, it may take possession of some organ formerly under the control of the waking personality and make it anesthetic, as with the hysteric. Or it may take over the waking life of an individual, alternating control with the ordinary self, as with multiple personality. Thus, Sidis sees all instances of the emergence of dissociated ideas or systems as a form of possession of the organism by the subwaking self.

Sidis also sees these intrusions by the subwaking self as a sort of plundering of the riches of the waking self. For no matter how personalized it may become, the subwaking self remains at bottom a brute, essentially lacking the psychological resources of the waking self.

Frederic Myers. Another researcher who affirmed that we all have a second, subconscious *self*—a self, however, very different from that postulated by Sidis—was the Englishman Frederic Myers. The work of Myers, one of the founders of the Society for Psychical Research, was of broad scope and of great relevance to the issue of dissociation. His master work, the posthumously published two-volume *Human Personality and Its Survival of Bodily Death,* appeared in 1903 and constitutes a massive compendium of information on that area.[18]

Out of his own investigation into dissociation phenomena and his extensive knowledge of the literature of the field, Myers eventually formulated a unique view of the nature of the subconscious, summarized in his notion of the "subliminal self."[19]

The subliminal self, Myers says, is the self "below the threshold" of consciousness. In contrast to the view of Sidis, Myers sees this subliminal self as the individual's main self, true self, or greater self. Myers holds that our ordinary consciousness, which he calls the supraliminal self (that *above* the threshold of consciousness), is simply a subordinate stream which has evolved from the subliminal self in order to exercise those capacities we need for existing in the world. As such, the supraliminal self is but a small fragment of the whole person, developed as the necessary means of living and evolving on this planet. It is the seat of one's ability to sense, think, solve practical problems, and adapt to the changing vicissitudes of everyday life. In this understanding of human personality, Myers tells us, "all subliminal action may be called automatism and regarded under the form of messages conveying information from the subliminal to the supraliminal self, in either a sensory or motor form."[20]

In Myers' conception of human personality, the subliminal self is the source of all faculties, lower and higher, operating outside our ordinary awareness. This means that it is both the source of the capacity to direct and modify at will our physiological functions, and also the seat of our highest intuitive powers. At the same time it is the repository of forgotten or suppressed memories and so can serve as a storehouse for split-off segments of experience which may become the seeds of hysterical symptoms or even full-blown alternate selves. These split-off segments can break through the threshold of consciousness into supraliminal awareness and manifest in the individual's ordinary life.

It is easy to see how Myers, using this paradigm of human personality, could explain everything from disintegrations of personality to flights of inspired genius. And that is exactly what he did in his two-volume *Human Personality and Its Survival of Bodily Death.*

Although *Human Personality* was a treatise on psychical research, Myers' viewpoint was preeminently psychological. William James, as a matter of fact, considered Myers to be one of the most remarkable psychological synthesizers of his day and stated that in his opinion Myers better than anyone else mapped out the crucial areas to be explored concerning the nature of the subconscious. James even went as far as to say that that inquiry ought to be designated "the problem of Myers."[21]

In *Human Personality* Myers produced an extensive treatment of the issues of dissociation drawn from sources in every language. The chapter headings of that work amount to an outline of the main divisions of dissociation, and in them we see a reflection of how the subject was viewed at the beginning of the century.[22] They are: Disintegrations of the Personality; Genius; Sleep and Dreams; Hypnotism; Sensory Automatism; Motor Automatism; and the more complete automatisms of Trance Phenomena, Possession, and Ecstasy.

It is not possible here even to summarize Myers' treatment of these areas. Let me just make one comment about the significance of his book. Its importance lies not only in the original perspective on the nature of the subconscious embodied in the concept of the subliminal self, but is also due to Myers' encyclopedic recapitulation of most of the previous work in the area. The two volumes contain more than 700 pages of appendices that summarize cases and present opinions ventured by investigators in the field. In the first chapter, where Myers discusses, among other things, somnambulisms and secondary personalities, he brings in a wealth of material from every possible source. As a matter of fact, his summary of cases of multiple personality was the most extensive in print up to that time, and remains a valuable resource for the investigator today.

Boris Sidis and Frederic Myers both attempted to synthesize the results of their own experiments with dissociation phenomena and the findings of others into a psychology of a subconscious *self*. Both wrote classical but now forgotten works on the subject: Sidis his *Psychology of Suggestion* and Myers his *Human Personality*. Each, however, came to very different formulations of the nature of the subconscious self. Sidis saw it more or less as a brutelike consciousness with a tendency toward personalization. Myers held that it included those functions and much more, being the source of all that is human, including the highest intuitive powers. With Myers and Sidis the theoretical exploration of dissociation and of the subconscious as a second self reached a certain logical extreme. They had moved about as far toward a psychological explanation of the phenomena as one could go.

The Freudian View of Dissociation

While debates about the physiology of dissociation and the existence of a subconscious self were going on, another controversy was brewing in the background. This was the conflict between the Freudian notion of the unconscious and the concept of the subconscious originating from Janet.

A scant three years after the publication of the "Symposium on the Subconscious" in the *Journal of Abnormal Psychology* there appeared in that same periodical another article on "The Conception of the Subconscious" by Bernard Hart.[23] Here Hart took up the notion of the unconscious as put forth by "Freud, Jung, and the Zurich School," and compared it to the Janetian view of the subconscious as developed in the earlier symposium. Sixteen years later Hart would complete his thought on the matter in an article that has become a classic, published in the *British Journal of Medical Psychology* and entitled: "The Conception of Dissociation."[24]

Hart's approach to his task is not to compare one psychological theory to another, to see whether Freud or Janet can make a stronger case for rival explanations for mental disturbance. So he does not involve us in a detailed analysis of the cogency of the elements of each system. His approach is more refreshing and intriguing than that. Hart attempts to show that in fact when speaking about the phenomena of dissociation, Freud and Janet are operating on two entirely different levels; in other words, what appear to be rival theories are in fact two different stages of inquiry.

It is Hart's contention that Janet's work on dissociation confines itself to the level of description of the phenomena, while Freud's concerns itself with conceptualization—that is, with construction of a theory. Here is how Hart works it out.

Hart begins by tackling the problem of the essential nature of Janet's description. He points out that basically Janet is always engaged in describing *conscious phenomena*. Whether he is describing the actions or communications of a primary personality or a secondary dissociated personality, he is always talking about a consciousness which manifests itself in a way we can *perceive,* whether by listening to it talk, reading its written communications, or watching its movements.

There is nothing unusual in this, says Hart. This is the way we normally come to know about conscious phenomena of all kinds. We have actual experience only of our own conscious phenomena and have to *deduce* the conscious phenomena of others, either directly through what they tell us or indirectly through watching their actions. So it is also with the phenomena of the subconscious. The distinction of the subconscious lies solely in the fact that it is dissociated from the main personality, and not for the reason that our knowledge of it is less direct than that of a primary consciousness. We do not use reason to come to awareness of the existence of a second consciousness in the individual any more than we use reason to come to awareness of the existence of the primary consciousness of another. We perceive them both equally through the direct evidence of our experience. Thus, Hart quotes Janet as saying that "the term 'doubling of consciousness' is not a philosophical explanation; it is a simple clinical observation of a common character which these phenomena present."[25]

But there are, says Hart, certain weaknesses in Janet's approach. For his concept of dissociation is constructed in terms of a spatial metaphor by which there is "a separation *en masse* of a number of mental elements from the greater aggregation of elements which constitutes the totality of mind, a splitting of the mind into two independent pieces."[26] This metaphor simply will not work to explain the presence of the same material in two or more dissociated systems. For example, each of two dissociated personalities may possess the same memories. Again it falls down in trying to account for such things as one-way amnesic barriers.

Hart's overall evaluation is that Janet is strong in his notion of dissociation and in his sketching out of the areas where the subconscious operates. These accomplishments stand in their own right, and the history of psychology will never be the same because of them. But Janet falters when it comes to *conceptualizing* or *theorizing* about the nonphenomenal source of the phenomena. His weakness is in assuming a spatial model for that unseen source, when in fact something much more subtle is needed. The spatial model could only regard dissociation as a breaking of the mind into many pieces and a dissociated system as an isolated buildup of psychic elements which in some cases could reach a mass of such dimensions that it could be called a personality. What is needed, says Hart, is a *functional* model for dissociation in which psychic elements could organize around different centers of synthesization, and in which the same elements could be part of more than one such synthesis: "Instead of regarding dissociation as the splitting of conscious material into separate masses, it must be regarded as an affair of gearing, the various elements of mental machinery being organized into different functional systems by the throwing in of the appropriate gear."[27]

Now it was Hart's contention that where Janet was weak, Freud was strong; that it was precisely in moving from the plane of the phenomenal to the conceptual that Freud had something important to offer. The conceptual model of the nonphenomenal structure of the human psyche put forward by Freud was original and intriguing. And it was embodied in his notion of the *Unbewusstsein,* the Unconscious. Freud's conception of the unconscious is not, says Hart, in competition with the subconscious of Janet. Janet's subconscious is the arena of dissociated phenomena which manifest in observable form as elements coactive with the personal self. Freud's unconscious is a conceptual, nonobservable construction put forward to explain certain facts of human experience. In this way Hart equates the unconscious with the atomic theory in physics or the theory of heredity in biology. Thus, the notions of the complex, the id, the ego, and the superego are constructions which, understood as dynamic but not directly observable constitutive elements, can make sense out of facts we *do* observe. As with all scientific constructs, says Hart, Freud's unconscious will stand or fall with its effectiveness in explaining observable data. By way of contrast, Janet's subconscious was little more than a description and categorization of observable phenomena. In this Hart credits Freud with the first consistent attempt to construct a conceptual psychology.

While Hart appreciated that Freud was undertaking an important scientific task, he believed that his conceptual model left something to be desired precisely with regard to the matter of dissociative phenomena. First of all he notes the conspicuous absence of double personality from psychoanalytic literature. There is, he asserts, little new case material of this kind coming from psychoanalysts, and they seem to suffer from a lack of interest in the whole matter. But in Hart's view it is not just the subject of multiple personality that is neglected, but the whole area of dissociation as it occurs on the phenomenal level. He then ventures an opinion as to why this is so:

The psycho-analyst has a line of approach altogether different from that followed by the investigators of multiple personality. The focus of his interest is not on the manifestations observed on the phenomenal plane, but on the dynamic factors conceived to lie behind them. The conflicting forces on this latter plane are the things that matter, and whether they manifest themselves on the phenomenal plane as one or other of various possible symptoms, or whether they lead to the complete splitting of double personality is of comparatively minor importance.[28]

Hart does, however, see in Freud's theorizing about the ego a possible contribution to our understanding of how dissociation originates:

In 'Das Ich und das Es' [Freud] states that the ego may be the subject of various identifications, and that, if these identifications are unusually strong and incompatible with one another, a splitting of the ego may occur; he then hazards the conjecture that the secret of cases of multiple personality may be that each of the various identifications alternately draws consciousness to itself.[29]

Hart ends his article on dissociation with a plea to psychoanalysts to give more thought to the problem. He says that he can sympathize with their sentiment that the phenomenal symptom is of secondary concern for one whose methodology is to tackle the problem of constructing an effective model on the conceptual plane. But, he concludes, "we should like to obtain from [the psychoanalysts] a dynamic interpretation of the facts which Janet and others of his school have observed, and among those facts the phenomena of dissociation and of double personality are surely worthy of note."[30]

When Hart ends with this good-natured plea to psychoanalysts, one cannot help wondering if he was well acquainted with what the founder of psychoanalysis had already written on the subject of dissociation in general and his disagreements with the views of Janet in particular. True, in 1909 Freud wrote in a manner that quite agreed with a central aspect of Hart's analysis. Describing Janet's view of dissociation Freud said:

According to him, hysteria is a form of degenerate modification of the nervous system, which shows itself in an innate weakness in the power of psychical synthesis. Hysterical patients, he believes, are inherently incapable of holding together the multiplicity of mental processes into a unity, and hence arises the tendency to mental dissociation. If I may be allowed to draw a homely but clear analogy, Janet's hysterical patient reminds one of a feeble woman who has gone out shopping and is now returning home laden with a multitude of parcels and boxes. She cannot contain the whole heap of them with her two arms and ten fingers. So first of all one object slips from her grasp; and when she stoops to pick it up, another one escapes her in its place, and so on. . . . I soon arrived at another view of the origin of hysterical dissociation (the splitting of consciousness).[31]

Freud then gives his more functional view of dissociation:

You will now see in what it is that the difference lies between our view and Janet's. We do not derive the psychical splitting from an innate incapacity for synthesis on the part of the mental apparatus; we explain it dynamically, from the conflict of opposing mental forces and recognize it as the outcome of an active struggling on the part of the two psychical groupings against each other.[32]

But by 1915 Freud had clearly pointed out that there was an even more fundamental difference between Janet's view and his own. It had to do with their very different understanding of the nature of the subconscious. In his treatise "The Unconscious" Freud said:

We shall . . . be right in rejecting the term "subconscious" as incorrect and misleading. The well-known cases of *"double conscience"* (splitting of consciousness) prove nothing against our view. We may most aptly describe them as cases of a splitting of the mental activities into two groups, and say that the same consciousness turns to one or other of these groups alternately. In psychoanalysis there is no choice for us but to assert that mental processes are in themselves unconscious, and to liken the perception of them by means of consciousness to the perception of the external world by means of the sense-organs.[33]

In denying the existence of a second consciousness, Freud was certainly doing more than merely working on a different level from that of Janet. He was directly contradicting him.

Janet himself seemed reluctant to admit that Freud's views were radically divergent from his own. In fact, he often tried to assert that Freud had simply taken over his own system and given it a new terminology. What Freud added beyond that, he said, was to transform, without sufficient basis, "a clinical observation and a treatment with a definite and limited field of use into an enormous system of medical philosophy."[34]

This dismissal of psychoanalysis was more than Freud could stomach, and by 1924 he was writing an angry rebuttal. It occurs in his

"Autobiographical Study" and provides us with a clearcut statement about how he saw dissociation. Freud first asserts that their very different views on that phenomenon should be enough to:

> put an end to the glib repetition of the view that whatever is of value in psychoanalysis is merely borrowed from the ideas of Janet. . . . I have always treated Janet himself with respect, . . . but when in the course of time psychoanalysis became a subject of discussion in France, Janet behaved ill, showed ignorance of the facts and used ugly arguments.[35]

He then goes on to make a point of what he had written earlier about the crucial difference in the way he and Janet view consciousness:

> Psycho-analysis regarded everything mental as being in the first instance unconscious; the further quality of 'consciousness' might also be present, or again it might be absent. This of course provoked a denial from the philosophers for whom 'conscious' and 'mental' were identical and who protested that they could not conceive of such an absurdity as the 'unconscious mental'. . . . It could be pointed out, incidently, that this was only treating one's own mental life as one had always treated other people's. One did not hesitate to ascribe mental processes to other people, although one had no immediate consciousness of them and could only infer them from their words and actions. But what held good for other people must be applicable to oneself. Anyone who tried to push the argument further and to conclude from it that one's own hidden processes belonged actually to a second *consciousness* would be faced with the concept of a consciousness of which one knew nothing, of an 'unconscious consciousness'—and this would scarcely be preferable to the assumption of an 'unconscious mental.' . . . The further question as to the ultimate nature of this unconscious is no more sensible or profitable than the older one as to the nature of the conscious.[36]

Thus for Freud dissociated systems are simply separate groups of mental but unconscious elements.[37] As our consciousness turns now to one group, now to another, as a searchlight shines now on one object and now on another, the dissociated groups manifest in conscious life. Of themselves the dissociated systems are mental in character, but not conscious. There exists no doubling of consciousness, no second consciousness.[38]

I would like to conclude this discussion of concepts of dissociation in the first half of the twentieth century with a brief reference to the view of Freud's erstwhile pupil, Carl Jung. We see in Jung's writings an understanding of dissociation phenomena much closer to that of Janet than of Freud. Indeed, like Janet, Jung made dissociation a key concept in his psychology.

Jung's approach is centered around the notion of the complex. A complex is an entity formed in the unconscious having an archetypal core clothed with the contents of personal experience of the individual. Jung sees the complex as a cohesive unity and sometimes refers to complexes as self-contained psyches within the big psyche. At other times he calls them fragmentary personalities dwelling inside us. Complexes give evidence of having a mind of their own, carrying on a kind of independent mental activity. It is in fact proper to say that complexes possess consciousness.[39]

Dissociation for Jung means being cut off from the ego, which is the center of an individual's field of consciousness. The ego is a source of unity for the person and the part which is "out there" dealing with the realities of the world.

Dissociated or autonomous complexes are those which have no direct association with the ego.[40] Though cut off from the ego, the dissociated complex will, if sufficiently charged with psychic energy, manifest in the life of the individual. This can happen in a number of ways. The dissociated complex may show itself in a neurotic symptom. It may be projected outside the individual and worshipped as a god or feared as a demon. Or it may burst forth from within and take possession of the waking life of an individual as an alternate personality. Therefore, a large part of Jungian therapy is aimed at the assimilation of dissociated complexes into the ego.

As mentioned, Jung considered each of the autonomous complexes to have a consciousness of its own. There are places where he goes further and speaks about the unconscious as having a unifying subject, and comes close to making the step taken by Sidis and Myers and positing a "subconscious self." I would like to bring my chapter to a close with his words on this matter:

If the unconscious can contain everything that is known to be a function of consciousness, then we are faced with the possibility that it too, like consciousness, possesses a subject, a sort of ego. This conclusion finds expression in the common and ever-recurring use of the term "subconsciousness." The latter term is certainly open to misunderstanding, as either it means what is "below consciousness," or it postulates a "lower" and secondary consciousness. At the same time this hypothetical "subconsciousness," which immediately becomes associated with a "superconsciousness," brings out the real point of my argument: the fact, namely, that a second psychic system coexisting with consciousness—no matter what qualities we suspect it of possessing—is of absolutely revolutionary significance in that it could radically alter our view of the world. Even if no more than the perceptions taking place in such a second psychic system were carried over into ego-consciousness, we should have the possibility of enormously extending the bounds of our mental horizon.[41]

Notes

1. Pierre Janet, "Les actes inconscients et la dédoublement de la personnalité pendant le somnambulisme provoqué," *Revue Philosophique* 22 (1886): 577–592; "L'anesthésie systématisée et la dissociation des phénomènes psychologiques," *Revue Philosophique* 23 (1887): 449–472; and "Les actes inconscients et la mémoire pendant le somnambulisme," *Revue Philosophique* 25 (1888): 238–279.
2. *L'automatisme psychologique.* Paris: Félix Alcan, 1889.
3. Janet, "Les actes inconscients et la mémoire," p. 277.
4. Pierre Janet, "A Symposium on the Subconscious," *Journal of Abnormal Psychology* 2 (1907): 58.
5. Janet, "A Symposium," p. 23.
6. See William Carpenter, *Principles of Mental Physiology,* 4th ed. London: Henry S. King, 1876, pp. 515–543; and *Nature and Man.* New York: D. Appleton, 1889, pp. 164–168, 261–315.
7. Hugo Münsterberg, "A Symposium on the Subconscious," *Journal of Abnormal Psychology* 2 (1907): 25–33. There was a strong emphasis on this view of dissociation among German authors of the day, as reflected by this definition of dissociation given by Edmund Parish in *Hallucinations and Illusions.* London: Walter Scott, 1897:

> By dissociation is here understood that state in which the nerve stimulus no longer flows through the channels determined by habit, and by the co-operation of simultaneous stimuli, because inhibitions, or obstructions, whether from pathological or physiological causes, have been set up in the normal association-paths, or obstructions which normally exist in other connecting tracts have been weakened or altogether abolished. (P. 152)

8. Münsterberg, "A Symposium," p. 32.
9. Morton Prince, "A Symposium on the Subconscious," *Journal of Abnormal Psychology* 2 (1907): 67–80.
10. Ibid., p. 69.
11. Ibid.

12. For example, *The Unconscious,* 2nd revised ed. New York: Macmillan, 1929, pp. 247ff.

13. Morton Prince, "Hysteria from the Point of View of Dissociated Personality," *Journal of Abnormal Psychology* 1 (1906): 172.

14. See the more complete edition: *The Dissociation of a Personality.* New York: Longmans, Green and Company, 1908.

15. In addition to Sidis and Myers, one could cite Max Dessoir, *Das Doppel-Ich,* 2nd ed. Leipzig: Ernst Günthers, 1896; and William James, *The Principles of Psychology.* New York: Henry Holt, 1890, vol. I, pp. 291–401.

16. Boris Sidis, *The Psychology of Suggestion.* New York: D. Appleton, 1911 (first edition 1898); *Psychopathological Researches.* New York: G. E. Stechert, 1902; *Symptomatology, Psychognosis, and Diagnosis of Psychopathic Diseases.* Boston: Richard G. Badger, 1914.

17. Sidis, *Psychology of Suggestion,* p. 296.

18. Frederic Myers, *Human Personality and Its Survival of Bodily Death,* 2 vols. London: Longmans, Green and Company, 1903.

19. For Myers' first formulation of his notion of the subliminal self, see his articles in the Society for Psychical Research *Proceedings:* "The Subliminal Consciousness," 7 (1892): 298–355; "The Subliminal Consciousness," 8 (1892): 436–535; "The Subliminal Consciousness," 9 (1893): 2–128; and "The Subliminal Self," 11 (1895): 334–593.

20. Myers, *Human Personality,* vol. I, p. xl.

21. William James, "In Memory of F. W. H. Myers," Society for Psychical Research *Proceedings,* 17 (1901): 13–18.

22. Myers's division of the subject bears some resemblance to that of William James as illustrated in the titles of his 1896 Lowell Lectures on "Exceptional Mental States": (1) Dreams and Hypnotism, (2) Automatism, (3) Hysteria, (4) Multiple Personality, (5) Demoniacal Possession, (6) Witchcraft, (7) Degeneration, and (8) Genius. We are indebted to Eugene Taylor for his careful reconstruction of these most interesting lectures. See Eugene Taylor, *William James on Exceptional Mental States: The 1896 Lowell Lectures.* New York: Scribners, 1983.

23. Bernard Hart, "The Conception of the Subconscious," *Journal of Abnormal Psychology* 4 (1910): 351–371.

24. Bernard Hart, "The Conception of Dissociation," *British Journal of Medical Psychology* 6 (1926): 241–263.

25. Janet, "A Symposium," p. 65.

26. Hart, "Conception of Dissociation," p. 243.

27. Ibid., p. 247.

28. Ibid., p. 255.

29. Ibid., p. 254.

30. Ibid., p. 256.

31. Sigmund Freud, "Five Lectures on Psychoanalysis" (1909), in *The Stan-*

dard Edition of the Complete Psychological Works of Sigmund Freud, ed. James Strachey. London: Hogarth Press, vol. XI, pp. 21–22.

32. Ibid., pp. 25–26.

33. Sigmund Freud, "The Unconscious" (1915), in *Standard Edition,* vol. XIV, pp. 170–171.

34. Pierre Janet, *Principles of Psychotherapy* as quoted in A. A. Roback, "Fifty Years of the Dissociation School," *Journal of Abnormal Psychology* 3 (1936): 133. See also, Pierre Janet, "Psychoanalysis," *Journal of Abnormal Psychology* 9 (1914): 1–35, 153–187; and Henri Ellenberger, *The Discovery of the Unconscious* (New York: Basic Books, 1970), p. 344.

35. Sigmund Freud, "An Autobiographical Study" (1925) in *Standard Edition,* vol. XX, p. 31.

36. Ibid., pp. 31–32.

37. William McDougall made some attempts to determine the relationship between dissociation and repression in the psychology of Freud. In his *Outline of Abnormal Psychology,* New York: Scribners, 1926, pp. 234–252, he distinguishes them in this way. Repression involves the forceful submergence of disturbing material which then reappears in distortions of feeling and response in the waking life of the individual. Though not consciously known to the person, the repressed material manifests symbolically through symptoms of mental disturbance. Dissociation involves the separation of a unit of experience from the awareness of the individual in such a way that the unit continues to exist subconsciously and may manifest as a unit in an automatism or somnambulism. It does not appear symbolically in everyday symptoms. Rather it emerges as a whole in episodes cut off from the awareness of the normal consciousness of the person. With repression, conscious exposure to the repressed material will cause agitation in the person. With dissociation, there is a lack of response to conscious exposure to the submerged material—a sort of unnatural indifference.

In an article written some 12 years later ("The Relations between Dissociation and Repression," *British Journal of Medical Psychology* 17 (1938): 141–157), McDougall returned to the subject with some additional thoughts. Here he says that to understand the relation of repression to dissociation we must distinguish between three different phenomena: disintegration, dissociation, and repression:

Dissociation is failure or imperfection of the associative mechanism or structure. Conflict and repression are affairs of the dynamic or moral relations between units. And when this latter system of dynamic relations breaks down, we get, in one form or another, not mere dissociation, but rather *disintegration.* . . . Perhaps it would be better to use *disharmony* as the descriptive term for such disorder of the dynamic relations; and to reserve the term 'disintegration' for those cases in which both kinds of disorder obtain, conflict and repression having led to severe dissociation (multiple personality). (P. 149)

38. It is strange to see that much later both A. A. Roback and William McDougall were still taking the old line that minimized the differences between Freud and Janet in this matter. See Roback, "Fifty Years of the Dissociation School," *Journal of Abnormal Psychology* 31 (1936): 131–137; and McDougall, "The Relations Between Dissociation and Repression," pp. 141–157.

39. Carl Jung, "Tavistock Lectures" (1935), in *The Collected Works of C. G. Jung,* Bollingen Series, vol. 18, p. 73; "Forward to Jung: 'Phénomènes Occultes'" (1939), in *Collected Works,* vol. 18, p. 309; "On the Nature of the Psyche" (1946), in *Collected Works,* vol. 8, pp. 174–175, 185–190; and "A Review of the Complex Theory" (1934), in *Collected Works,* vol. 8, pp. 96ff.

40. Carl Jung, "The Psychological Foundations of Belief in Spirits" (1919), in *Collected Works,* vol. 8, p. 309.

41. Carl Jung, "On the Nature of the Psyche" (1946), in *Collected Works,* vol. 8, pp. 177–178.

5. The Scientific Investigation of Multiple Personality Disorder

Frank W. Putnam, M.D.

Historical Review

The history of multiple personality disorder (MPD) as a clinical syndrome spans the development of modern psychiatry.[1] Interest in and acceptance of this disorder has waxed and waned over the last century. This fluctuation of interest in MPD may reflect changes in the popularity of hypnosis as a diagnostic and therapeutic tool,[2] the criticism of Morton Prince and other prominent investigators of the disorder as charlatans or at best as unwitting dupes of their patients,[1] and the rise of schizophrenia as a diagnostic entity in the early part of this century.[3]

We are again in a period of renewed interest in multiple personality disorder and allied dissociative reactions. Our interest in MPD as a psychiatric disorder and as a window into the organization of consciousness is clear from the dramatic increase in the number of case reports, theoretical articles, and symposia that have appeared in the last decade.[4] This chapter will focus on the emerging scientific investigation of multiple personality, both as a distinct clinical entity and as a powerful model for probing many of the salient issues of modern psychiatry. We will consider the problems to be investigated, the tools at our disposal, and models or paradigms which can provide a framework within which specific questions can be asked.

Nineteenth-century philosophers, psychologists, and physicians were intrigued by the phenomena of double consciousness and multiple personality. Charcot, Janet, and Ribot each offered explanations for these phenomena which can still serve as paradigms for scientific investigation today. Since the earliest cases, clinicians have reported witnessing unusual physiological changes in MPD patients accompanying the alternation of personalities. Morton Prince was the first investigator to attempt scientifically to document the reported physiological manifestations of alternate personalities. He had observed that his celebrated patient, Miss Beauchamp, a young preparatory school student with several personalities, demonstrated marked changes between two of her personalities, which he designated B IV and B I. "She (B IV) had individual peculiarities of character, of disposition, of temperament, of tastes, of habits, of memory, and of physical health, which sharply distinguished her from B I. Even many of her physiological reactions to the environment were different."[5]

Prince, together with Frederick Peterson, a professor of psychiatry at Columbia University, sought to verify the existence of an alternate personality.[6] They employed a galvanometer and kymograph to measure changes in galvanic skin resistance to emotionally laden stimulus words embedded within a list of neutral words. Prince sought to exploit experimentally one of the most frequently observed clinical facts about MPD patients, directional awareness. Therapists working with these patients find that some of the alternate personalities report being able to see and hear everything that occurs when another personality is in control of the body. These alternate personalities are said to be coconscious. Other alternate personalities report no awareness of what transpires when they are not "out" and manifest amnesia for these periods. Over 85 percent of the clinicians surveyed in a National Institute of Mental Health (NIMH) questionnaire study report seeing evidence of this directional consciousness in their MPD patients.[7]

Prince concluded that the galvanic responses to embedded emotionally charged words were ". . . compatible with and, so far, confirmatory of the theory that these subconscious processes are psychical (coconscious)." No clear conclusions can be drawn from Prince and Peterson's uncontrolled study, but the design and the utilization of the clinically observed directional awareness have been employed in recent studies of MPD.[8]

The diagnosis of MPD fell into disrepute shortly thereafter. Prince and other investigators were roundly criticized by McDougall and other prominent psychologists as having produced the personalities that they were observing.[1] Sporadic investigations into dissociation continued during the 1920s and 1930s using hypnosis as a model. Ramona Messerschmidt, under the direction of Clark Hull, carried out a series of investigations on the interference of "conscious" and "subconscious" tasks which showed greater interference in the hypnotic condition than in the normal waking state.[9] These studies, together with others which also refuted the non-interference model of dissociation, led to a decline in interest in MPD both clinically and experimentally.[10]

Nevertheless, occasional case reports of MPD continued to appear in the literature throughout the 1930s and 1940s. In 1954, Thigpen and Cleckley first reported on the now famous case of *The Three Faces of Eve*. They attempted to document differences among the three personalities using the electroencephalogram (EEG) and reported that they found differences in muscle tension among all of the personalities and differences in alpha background frequency of 1.5 Hz between two of the alternate personalities.[11] In 1953, Morselli described finding similar EEG differences in his MPD patient, Marisa.[12] Condon et al. made a frame-by-frame study of a 30-minute film of four of Eve's personalities. They report detecting differences in three types of eye movements across the personalities.[13]

The number of case reports of MPD underwent a dramatic increase beginning about 1972, a trend which continues to accelerate.[4] During the 1970s, Ludwig et al. conducted a series of physiological studies on two patients, Jonah and Faith.[14,15] They attempted to discern differences among the alternate personalities using psychological testing; electroencephalography (EEG); visual evoked potentials; and with Jonah, using a galvanic skin response experiment that was very similar to Morton Prince's design. They found differences in muscle tension, alpha blocking and modal alpha frequency, which they felt represented "real physiological differences" and were not simply due to changes in attention and arousal. Bahnson and Smith also reported on a multiple personality patient, whom they followed through therapy with electrocardiogram and galvanic skin response recordings. They noted personality-specific GSR responsivity to therapeutic interventions.[16]

The 1980s have seen the beginning of the first systematically controlled investigations into the psychophysiology of multiple personality disorder. Coons et al. did a frequency analysis over six pairs of EEG leads on two MPD patients, together with a simulating control subject.[17] They found that both the simulating control and the two MPD patients exhibited significant changes across alternate personalities. The control subject and the multiple personality patients differed in which frequency bands showed significant differences, but the control demonstrated a greater total number of differences. They concluded that these differences were probably due to changes in concentration, mood, and muscle tension.

Putnam et al. reported on a study comparing the P_{100}, N_{120}, and P_{200} components of the visual evoked response in 11 MPD patients and ten matched control subjects.[18] The age- and gender-matched control subjects created and practiced alternate personalities, who were handled experimentally in the same manner as the patient's alternate personalities. Each alternate personality was tested on five separate days in a randomized order. Intraclass correlation coefficients were then calculated for each group and compared by the method of Fisher. The multiple personality patients had significantly lower intraclass correlation coefficients than the control subjects, indicating that the MPD alternate personalities looked significantly less like each other on the measures of amplitude and latency for the P_{100}, N_{120}, and P_{200} visually evoked potential components than did the "alternate personalities" of the simulating control subjects.

A number of uncontrolled experimental studies have also appeared recently. Brende has described the measurement of galvanic skin responses among three personalities of a MPD patient and speculates that the observed GSR desynchronization between the left and right sides of the body may reflect hemispheric dissociation.[19] Braun has published a preliminary report of neurophysiological changes in two multiple personality patients with integration achieved through hypnotherapy.[20] Both of these studies lack a control group so that, while the reported findings are interesting, it remains unclear as to whether or not these results represent significant physiological changes or merely normal variation over time.

Research Issues

The Questions. The question that is inevitably asked of multiple personality disorder is: "Is it real?"[21] To date, most investigators have tried implicitly or explicitly to determine if MPD is real by seeking to find some measure on which alternate personalities of the same MPD patient are as different as two separate individuals. Despite claims in the lay press to the contrary, no scientific study to date has succeeded in proving the existence of MPD by this criterion. Nor is any study likely to in the near future, since, with the exception of physical differences such as fingerprints, there are few if any physiological or psychological measures which can reliably distinguish separate individuals from one another. The implicit pressure to find scientific proof of the existence of MPD is unique within the field of psychiatry, where all other diagnoses are made by clinical consensus. Scientific studies directed solely at attempting to prove or disprove the existence of multiple personality disorder, particularly using the above criterion, are not likely to succeed or to shed much light on the nature of multiple personality disorder. Instead, we should approach the study of MPD in much the same manner as any other psychiatric disorder, moving from an initial descriptive phase into a correlative phase and finally into an active experimental investigation of the pathologic mechanisms involved.

The scientific study of multiple personality disorder began with investigations centered around single cases. We need to expand this narrow focus and to acquire a broader perspective on the disorder using traditional epidemiological methodology. At this point, we do not know which among the many unusual phenomena anecdotally reported to be associated with multiple personality disorder are idiosyncratic to specific cases and which are universally associated with the disorder. There are continually increasing estimates of the incidence and prevalence of the disorder, but all of these current estimates are based on the informal compilation of cases known to the investigators directly or through their contacts. As yet, there has been no systematic study to determine the incidence of this disorder in the general population. The work of Bliss and his collaborators on hypnotizability and MPD within defined psychiatric populations is a first step.[22]

The relationship of multiple personality disorder to other psychiatric disorders remains to be defined. Some authors, for example, have suggested that MPD is a variant of borderline personality disorder.[23] Other authors report an overlap of core borderline features by standard criteria in up to 70% of their MPD cases, but note that some MPD patients would not meet traditional criteria for borderline personality disorder.[24,25] The relationship of multiple personality disorder to temporal lobe epilepsy is an example of another overlap that may be coincidental or causal and requires further clarification.[26,27]

Are there subtypes of multiple personality disorder patients? Experienced therapists tend to think so, and often speak of simple vs. complex MPD patients. There is some evidence that those patients with more alternate personalities have more self-destructive and sociopathic behavior and may be more difficult to treat.[7] These and other questions related to the incidence and general clinical phenomenology of multiple personality disorder deserve systematic inquiry.

Treatment and outcome of MPD is yet another important area that is in need of scientific scrutiny. A wide variety of different therapeutic interventions, ranging from ECT to "re-parenting psychotherapy," have been tried for MPD. Success has been claimed for many of them at some point. Until Kluft articulated his criteria for "fusion," no standard existed by which to define and compare the integration of alternate personalities into a single unified personality, an often-claimed endpoint for successful treatment of the disorder.[24] Standardized evaluation of a variety of treatment modalities, ranging from pharmacotherapies with antidepressants, anticonvulsants, anxiolytics, and antipsychotics, to hypnotherapy, is necessary to determine the range of appropriate therapeutic interventions for multiple personality disorder.

The linkage of multiple personality disorder to childhood trauma is an extraordinarily cogent research issue to be pursued. Virtually all of the modern reviewers of this syndrome have concluded that childhood trauma, particularly childhood physical and sexual abuse, is directly involved in the etiology of this disorder.[28] The implications of this reported connection between MPD and childhood trauma for understanding the long-term effects of traumatic experiences and the interaction of traumatic experiences with development are profound and would be applicable in many other areas of psychiatry and human psychology.

The research questions that investigators find the most intriguing, however, are the mind/body issues raised by the alternate personalities. Do they really have different bodily physiologies? What does this say about the influence of "personality" on the body, the nature of personality, or the structure of consciousness? Theories abound, but presently very little factual information is available. There are numerous anecdotes of observed physiological differences among alternate personalities of individuals with MPD. These observations include changes in handedness; different responses to medications, drugs, or alcohol; different allergic sensitivities; and different somatic symptoms.[18] The relatively large number of reports of physiological changes across alternate personalities compared to the total number of reported cases in the literature suggests that indeed something unusual is happening with these patients. The degree to which these observed physiological changes are unique to multiple personality disorder remains, however, to be determined.

The Methodologies Available to Study MPD. All of the modern techniques and technologies that are being applied to the study of psychiatric illness in general are available for the study of multiple personality disorder. A few words of caution, however, are in order. The last few years have seen a dramatic increase in the number of new technologies available for research into the mind and the body. These include: computerized axial tomography (CAT scans), radioisotope studies such as the xenon-inhalation brain scans (rCBF), computerized topographic electroencephalograms and evoked potential topographic mapping (BEAM), positron emission tomography (PET), nuclear magnetic resonance scans (NMR) and the magneotoencephalogram (MEG), to name a few. The development of these new technologies and their application to research in psychiatry and medicine is occurring at a faster rate than we can comprehend and assimilate. In many cases, sufficient numbers of normal subjects have not been studied, so that we really do not know which findings represent normal variants and which are secondary to pathology. If we recall that it has been over half a century since Hans Berger discovered the EEG and first described the alpha rhythm, and yet there still remains significant disagreement over what this fundamental neural activity represents, then we can appreciate the enormous task of understanding and incorporating these new technologies that lies before us.

In general, a few principles are worth noting when attempting to apply these new technologies to research with MPD patients. The testing period should be limited to 15–20 minutes or less, which is generally the upper limit that many alternate personalities can "hold the body" in a stressful situation before a spontaneous switch to another alternate personality occurs. The test needs to be repeatable several times to allow for the study of several alternate personalities within a short period. Certain technologies, e.g. PET scans or other isotope studies, that require high levels of radiation for imaging, limit the repeatability of the test. The methodology should have well-established norms for normal controls and specific pathologies so that any changes seen with alternate personalities can be interpreted within a broader context. And finally, the testing situations should not be too frightening or confining. When working with MPD patients, the investigator should always be aware of the fact that he/she is working with a group of highly traumatized subjects who may find the laboratory situation reminiscent of a past abusive context which may evoke a vivid abreaction.

Many of these new technologies provide dazzling computerized graphical representations of the results. But seeing should not be believing, and appropriate statistical analysis of the numeric data remains the tool for determining the significance of findings. In multiple personality disorder, the appropriate statistical methodology can be tricky and much remains to be worked out. The standard statistical tests were developed to determine the degree of difference between groups or the same person under different conditions. The applicability of these statistical tests to experiments involving alternate personalities needs to be clarified.

The choice of appropriate control groups against which to compare MPD patients is also a complex question. The first studies have tended to use groups of simulating control subjects who create and act out "alternate personalities," who were treated in the same fashion as the MPD alternate personalities. One criticism of this method focuses on the competence or skill of the simulating controls. Are they comparable "actors" to the MPD patients, who have had longer to "rehearse" their alternate personalities? Future control groups should include subjects who alter their state of consciousness in other fashions, perhaps through hypnosis or medication. Psychiatric patients, such as manic-depressives or premenstrual tension syndrome patients, who periodically cycle through replicable mood states, may also serve as appropriate control groups for some studies.

In the actual day-to-day work of research on MPD, experimental method issues frequently arise that further complicate the study of this disorder. These problems are too numerous and situation-specific to be addressed in this paper, but include issues such as: informed consent, the identification of which alternate personalities are actually taking part in a study, recognition of uncontrolled switching of alternate personalities, dealing with abreactions and other sometimes violent behaviors, and controlling for practice effects when testing several alternate personalities in the same patient.[21]

Models of Multiple Personality Disorder

According to Einstein, the purpose of a model or theory was to "make the chaotic diversity of our sense experience correspond to a logically uniform system of thought by correlating single experiences with the theoretic structure."[29]

Trance State Models. The relationship between multiple personality disorder and hypnosis was first commented on by Janet in 1889 and subsequently elaborated by Morton Prince in 1890.[30,31] Prince suggested that if a patient were "hypnotized sufficiently often and under sufficiently varied circumstances, the conscious experiences of her second self . . . would become extensive." Hypnosis and the trait of hypnotizability have remained a focus of interest among investigators of MPD.[22]

Four lines of circumstantial evidence suggest that a linkage exists between hypnosis and MPD. The first is the frequent observation that MPD patients in general are highly hypnotizable. Putnam et al. found that 73% of clinicians using hypnosis with their MPD patients ranked them as highly hypnotizable relative to their other patients.[7] Bliss has systematically scaled MPD patients using the Stanford Hypnotic Susceptibility Scale and found that the MPD patients were near the top end with a mean score of 10 ± 0.37 compared to the control subjects' mean score of 5.2 ± 0.18 ($P < 0.001$).[22] The second line of evidence is that many of the clinical symptoms seen in MPD patients can be induced under hypnosis in highly hypnotizable subjects. This includes posthypnotic amnesia for events occurring in the trance state, which has many similarities to the amnesia seen among alternate personalities in MPD patients. Conversion reactions and auditory and visual hallucinations, which are common in MPD,[7] can be created by suggestion in highly hypnotizable subjects. The phenomena seen with hypnotic age-regression have been equated with the child alternate personalities that are commonly found in MPD patients.

The third factor suggesting a connection between MPD and hypnosis involves the linkage to traumatic experiences. Hypnotically induced abreactions have long been used to treat traumatic neuroses, particularly in wartime dissociative reactions.[28] According to three independent studies,[32,33,34] hypnotizability in adults is best correlated with a childhood history of "strict" discipline and punishment. Trance-like behavior in children has been found to be the single best predictor of childhood multiple personality disorder.[35] The fourth line of evidence linking hypnosis and MPD is a number of studies in which "multiple personalitylike" phenomena have been created in normal subjects using hypnosis.[36,37] The hypnotically created "alternate personalities" as described in these studies lack much of the depth of the alternate personalities of MPD patients and are not true analogues of MPD, but suggest that personality-like phenomena may be evokable by hypnosis given sufficient time and motivation.

Temporal Lobe Dysfunction Model of MPD. In 1892, Charcot suggested that there was a link between multiple personality disorder and epilepsy.[38] Over the ensuing years, clinicians have continued to report the coexistence of epilepsy and multiple personality disorder.[26,27] The NIMH clinician's questionnaire survey on multiple personality disorder revealed that 20% of MPD patients who had received an EEG as part of their diagnostic workup had abnormalities reported.[7] This is at

Table 5.1 A Comparison of Symptoms in MPD Patients with Normal and Abnormal EEGs

Symptoms	Abnormal EEG (%) (n=11)	Normal EEG (%) (n=45)
Depression	91	91
Suicide attempt	82	72
Amnesia	73	98
Fugue episodes	73	56
Chronic depersonalization	45	58
Conversion reactions	55	67
Visual hallucinations	45	30
Auditory hallucinations	73	31
Tactile hallucinations	82	21
Olfactory hallucinations	82	12

Table 5.2 A Comparison of Alternate Personality Attributes in MPD Patients with Normal and Abnormal EEGs

Attribute	Abnormal EEG (%) (n=11)	Normal EEG (%) (n=45)
Child	73	78
Opposite-gender	73	58
Unaware of other alternates	82	78
Violent	91	79
Internal persecutor	73	53
Different handedness	36	38

least twice as frequent as would be expected by chance. The most commonly reported abnormality is bilateral temporal lobe slowing. A comparison of MPD patients with abnormalities in their EEG and MPD patients with normal EEGs reveals few differences in their clinical symptoms, alternate personality attributes, or childhood histories for traumatic experiences (see tables 5.1, 5.2 and 5.3).

Table 5.1 compares representative symptoms between these two groups. MPD patients with EEG abnormalities have a higher incidence of hallucinatory experiences, particularly tactile and olfactory hallucinations, than MPD patients with normal EEGs.

Table 5.2 compares representative personality attributes between MPD patients with normal and abnormal EEGs. There are essentially no differences between the frequency of these attributes in the two groups. It is worth noting that the likelihood of finding alternate

Table 5.3 A Comparison of the Reported Childhood History in MPD Patients with Normal and Abnormal EEGs

Reported History	Abnormal EEG (%) (n=11)	Normal EEG (%) (n=45)
Incest	67	68
Physical abuse	80	82
Single episode of sexual abuse	25	21

personalities with differences in dominant handedness is the same across the two groups. If shifts in dominant handedness across alternate personalities reflect a change in hemispheric dominance, then this phenomenon occurs equally frequently in MPD patients with EEG evidence of neurologic abnormality and those without this marker.

Table 5.3 compares the reported childhood history of MPD patients with and without abnormal EEGs. There is no difference in terms of a retrospectively reported history of childhood traumatic experiences between these two groups.

There is embedded within the neurologic literature a number of case reports of duality of consciousness in patients with epilepsy. Hughlings Jackson spoke of this as "mental diplopia" and Wilder Penfield described it as "doubling of consciousness."[39] This phenomenon is most often found in patients with right-sided epileptic foci.[26,39] The incidence of depersonalization in these epileptic patients with a doubling of consciousness is 44%, which is the same as in MPD patients with EEG abnormalities and similar to the incidence in MPD patients in general.[7,39]

A possible neurobiological model that could be invoked to explain multiple personality disorder is kindling. This phenomenon was first reported by Goddard and Morrell, who described the behavioral sensitization and convulsive response that occurs when an animal is subjected to a repeated stimulus over a period of time.[40] The limbic structures of the central nervous system (CNS), particularly the amygdala, are the most sensitive to kindling stimuli.[41] Kindling has been shown to occur with electrical stimulation of the CNS, interperitoneal lidocaine injections, and environmental stress.[41] Kindling has been proposed as a model for alcohol withdrawal seizures,[42] cocaine psychosis,[43] and affective illness.[44] In the case of multiple personality disorder, the kindling stimuli would be the repeated childhood sexual and physical abuse that has been reported to occur in the vast majority of MPD patients.[28] This repeated abuse generally occurs during the developmentally vulnerable period of age 6 months to 12 years when the child is undergoing development and maturation of psychological and physiological processes involved in the regulation of emotion and identity.[28] A hypothesis has been advanced that children between these ages are particularly likely to use dissociative mechanisms for coping with stress.[28]

In a kindling model, multiple personality disorder would be viewed as an epileptic equivalent which was produced over time through repeated sensitization by abusive experiences during a developmentally vulnerable period in childhood. In some MPD patients, a full-fledged seizure disorder is manifest; in other MPD patients a cortical/temporal lobe dysfunction occurs, which may or may not be detectable clinically, and gives rise to experiences of depersonalization and multiplicity of consciousness.

State Dependent Learning Model of MPD. In 1891, Ribot proposed the first theoretical formulation of state dependent learning (SDL) to account for cases of dual personality and somnambulistic states.[45] He stressed the importance of bodily sensations, physiologic states, and other organic cues as necessary to access certain memories in an individual. State dependent learning remained an obscure phenomenon, known primarily through the repeated citation in texts of a small number of celebrated clinical vignettes, until the experimental demonstrations of Girden using classically conditioned responses in dogs.[46] In the last 20 years, SDL has been the subject of over 100 investigations in animals and approximately 50 investigations in human subjects. These studies indicate that SDL is a general phenomenon that can be seen across a range of experimental paradigms in a number of species and produced by a variety of drugs.[46] The current emphasis in SDL studies is on drug discrimination (DD) phenomena.[46]

State dependent learning has again been proposed as a model to understand the amnesic barriers that appear to exist among certain alternate personalities in MPD patients. These amnesic barriers, together with the directional awareness phenomena described above, could constitute examples of cued memory accessibility, where the cues are provided by the physiological and psychological correlates of the alternate personalities. The physiologic studies reviewed above suggest that there are some physiologic correlates, primarily muscle tension, that seem to distinguish the alternate personalities from each other. These correlates could act to code memory storage, particularly traumatic memories, in such a fashion that they would be most readily retrieved when the individual reentered a similar state. In addition, new experiences acquired in a specific state defined by the physiological correlates of an alternate personality would be most accessible in that state and would be less retrievable in other alternate personality states.

One study that lends support to an SDL model of amnesic barriers in

MPD was performed by Silberman et al.[8] They found that two distinct lists of highly similar words, learned within and across alternate personalities of MPD patients and simulating control subjects, were recalled separately significantly better by alternate personalities of MPD patients who reported being amnesic for each other, than by a single alternate personality or across the "alternate personalities" of the simulating control subjects. There was no difference in the number of words recalled, indicating that the MPD patients and controls had equivalent ability to learn and remember the word lists, but mutually amnesic alternate personalities could keep the highly similar word lists segregated, whereas the simulating control subjects manifested a significant degree of "leakage" across their sham alternate personalities.

Summary

The scientific investigation of multiple personality disorder is just in its infancy, with the first controlled studies occurring within the last few years. A great deal of basic work needs to be done. Clinical studies on phenomenology, treatment, and outcome remain to be initiated. Recent physiological studies on the differences among alternate personalities suggest that differences do exist and may provide us with a unique opportunity to tease apart many of the psychosomatic issues that have plagued psychiatry. The implied linkage between the traumatic childhood experiences of MPD patients and their subsequent major dissociative psychopathology also provides us with a model that can illuminate psychodynamic and developmental issues in psychiatry. A variety of powerful technologies and methodologies are available and can be applied to the study of MPD, but they must be understood and used with rigor. The models with which we conceptualize MPD and against which we compare our results have roots which extend back to the beginnings of modern psychiatry.

Notes

1. H. F. Ellenberger, *The Discovery of the Unconscious: The History and Evolution of Dynamic Psychiatry*. New York: Basic, 1970.
2. E. L. Bliss, "Multiple Personalities: A Report of 14 Cases with Implications for Schizophrenia and Hysteria," *Arch. Gen. Psychiat.* 37 (1980): 1388–1397.

3. M. Rosenbaum, "The Role of the Term Schizophrenia in the Decline of Diagnoses of Multiple Personality," *Arch. Gen. Psychiat.* 37 (1980): 1383–1385.

4. M. Boor and P. M. Coons, "A Comprehensive Bibliography of Literature Pertaining to Multiple Personality," *Psychol. Reports* 53 (1983): 295–310.

5. M. Prince, *The Dissociation of a Personality.* New York: Longman, 1906.

6. M. Prince and F. Peterson, "Experiments in Psychogalvanic Reactions from Co-Conscious Ideal in a Case of Multiple Personality," *J. Abnorm. Psychol.* 3 (1908): 114–131.

7. F. W. Putnam, R. M. Post, and J. J. Guroff et al., "100 Cases of Multiple Personality Disorder," presented at the Annual Meeting of the American Psychiatric Association, New research abstract no. 77, 1983.

8. E. K. Silberman, F. W. Putnam, H. Weingartener, and R. M. Post, "Dissociative States in Multiple Personality Disorder: A Quantitative Study," presented at the Annual Meeting of the American Psychiatric Association, symposium: *Multiple Personality Disorder: A Psychophysiologic Illness,* May 1984.

9. R. A. Messerschmidt, "A Quantitative Investigation of the Alleged Independent Operation of Conscious and Subconscious Processes," *J. Abnorm. Soc. Psychol.* 22 (1927): 325–340.

10. E. R. Hilgard, *Divided Consciousness: Multiple Controls in Human Thought and Action.* New York: Wiley, 1977.

11. C. H. Thigpen and H. Cleckley, "A Case of Multiple Personality," *J. Abnorm. Soc. Psychol.* 49 (1954): 135–151.

12. G. E. Morselli, "Personalities alternate e patologic affecttiva," *Arch. Psychol. Neurol. Psichiatria,* 14 (1953): 579–589.

13. W. S. Condon, W. D. Ogston, and L. V. Pacoe, "Three Faces of Eve Revisited: A Study of Transient Microstrabismus," *J. Abnorm. Psychol.* 74 (1969): 618–620.

14. A. M. Ludwig, J. Brandsma and C. Wilbur et al. "The Objective Study of a Multiple Personality," *Arch. Gen. Psychiat.* 26 (1972): 298–310.

15. K. Larmore, A. M. Ludwig, and R. L. Cain, "Multiple Personality: An Objective Case Study," *Brit. J. Psychiat.* 131 (1977): 35–40.

16. C. B. Bahnson and K. Smith, "Autonomic Changes in a Multiple Personality," *Psychosomatic Med.* 37 (1975): 85–86.

17. P. M. Coons, V. Milstein, and C. Marley, "EEG Studies of Two Multiple Personalities and a Control," *Arch. Gen. Psychiat.* 39 (1982): 823–825.

18. F. W. Putnam, M. Buchsbaum, F. Howland, B. G. Braun, and R. M. Post, "Evoked Potentials in Multiple Personality Disorder," presented at the Annual Meeting of the American Psychiatric Association, *New Research Abstract #137,* 1982.

19. J. O. Brende, "The Psychophysiologic Manifestations of Dissociation," *Psych. Clinics of N. Am.* 7 (1984): 41–50.

20. B. G. Braun, "Neurophysiologic Changes Due to Integration: A Preliminary Report," *Am. J. Clin. Hypn.* 26 (1983): 84–92.

21. F. W. Putnam, "The Study of Multiple Personality Disorder: General Strategies and Practical Considerations," *Psychiat. Annals* 14 (1984): 58–61.

22. E. L. Bliss, "Multiple Personalities, Related Disorders and Hypnosis," *Am. J. Clin. Hypn.* 26 (1983): 114–123.

23. W. F. Clary, K. J. Burstin and J. S. Carpenter, "Multiple Personality and Borderline Personality Disorder," *Psych. Clinics of N. Am.* 7 (1984): 69–88.

24. R. P. Kluft, "Treatment of Multiple Personality Disorder: A Study of 33 Cases," *Psych. Clinics of N. Am.* 7 (1984): 9–29.

25. R. P. Horevitz and B. G. Braun, Are Multiple Personalities Borderline? *Psych. Clinics of N. Am.* 7 (1984): 69–88.

26. M. M. Mesulam, "Dissociative States with Abnormal Temporal Lobe EEG: Multiple Personality and the Illusion of Possession," *Arch. Neurol.* 38 (1981): 176–181.

27. L. Schenk and D. Bear, "Multiple Personality and Related Dissociative States in Patients with Temporal Lobe Epilepsy," *Am. J. Psychiat.* 138 (1981): 1311–1316.

28. F. W. Putnam, "Dissociation as a Response to Extreme Stress," in R. P. Kluft, ed., *Childhood Antecedents of Multiple Personality*. Washington: American Psychiatric Association, in press.

29. K. M. Colby, *Artificial Paranoia*. New York: Pergamon Press, 1975.

30. P. Janet, *L'automatisme psycholoque*. Paris: Pans Baillière, 1889.

31. M. Prince, "Some of the Revelations of Hypnotism," *Bost. Med. Surg. J.,* 122 (1890): 463–467.

32. D. P. Nowlis, "The Child-Rearing Antecedents of Hypnotic Susceptibility and of Naturally Occurring Hypnotic-Like Experience," *Int. J. Clin. Hyp.* 17 (1969): 109–120.

33. E. R. Hilgard, *Personality and Hypnosis: A Study of Imaginative Involvement*. Chicago: University of Chicago Press, 1970.

34. L. M. Cooper and P. London, "Children's Hypnotic Susceptibility, Personality and EEG Patterns," *Int. J. Clin. Hyp.* 24 (1976): 140–148.

35. R. P. Kluft, "Multiple Personality in Childhood," *Psych. Clinics of N. Am.,* 7 (1984): 121–134.

36. P. L. Harriman, "The Experimental Production of Some Phenomena Related to Multiple Personality," *J. Abnorm. Soc. Psychol.* 37 (1942): 244–255.

37. R. Kampman, "Hypnotically Induced Multiple Personality: An Experimental Study," *Int. J. Clin. Exper. Hypn.* 24 (1976): 215–227.

38. J. M. Charcot and P. Marie, "On Hysteroepilepsy," in H. Tuke, ed., *A Dictionary of Psychological Medicine*. London: Churchill, 1892.

39. S. Kamiya and S. Okamoto, "Double Consciousness in Epileptics: A Clinical Picture and Minor Hemispheric Specialization," in H. Akimoto, M. Kazamatsuri, M. Seino, and A. Ward, ed., *Advances in Epileptology: XIIIth Epilepsy International Symposium*. New York: Raven Press, 1982.

40. G. V. Goddard and F. Morrell, "Chronic Progressive Epileptogenesis Induced by Focal Electrical Stimulation of the Brain," *Neurology* 21 (1971): 393–397.
41. R. M. Post, T. W. Uhde, and F. W. Putnam et al., "Kindling and Carbamazepine in Affective Illness," *J. Nerv. Ment. Dis.* 170 (1982): 7–43.
42. R. M. Post, T. W. Uhde, F. W. Putnam, and W. E. Bunney, "Carbamazepine in Alcohol Withdrawal Syndromes: Relationship to the Kindling Model," *J. Clin. Psychopharm.* 3 (1983): 204–205.
43. R. M. Post and R. T. Kopanda, "Cocaine, Kindling and Psychosis," *Am. J. Psychiat.* 133 (1976): 627–634.
44. R. M. Post, J. C. Ballenger, T. W. Uhde, F. W. Putnam, and W. E. Bunney, "Kindling and Drug Sensitization: Implications for the Progressive Development of Psychopathology and Treatment with Carbamazepine," in M. Sandler, ed., *The Psychopharmacology of Anticonvulsants.* Oxford: Oxford University Press, 1981.
45. T. Ribot, *The Diseases of Personality.* Chicago: Open Court Publishing, 1891.
46. D. A. Overton, "State Dependent Learning and Drug Discriminations," in L. L. Iverson, S. D. Iverson, and S. H. Snyder, *Handbook of Psychopharmacology,* vol. 18. New York: Plenum, 1984.

6. Can Neurological Disconnection Account for Psychiatric Dissociation?

John J. Sidtis, Ph.D.

What is the cause of the defective integration of thought and behavior found in dissociative phenomena? If one were to look for a neurological model, the question might be posed more specifically: Does neurological disconnection produce psychiatric dissociation? Both neurological disconnection and psychiatric dissociation imply an uncoupling; in the former case the uncoupling occurs between brain areas, while in the latter case the uncoupling occurs between behaviors or psychological states. In this chapter, the changes associated with one of the most significant neurological disconnections, the so-called "split-brain" syndrome, will be reviewed, as will studies on the functional independence of the two hemispheres, and the degree to which the split-brain can serve as a model for dissociative phenomena.

Neurological disconnection can occur in many ways, but those of interest for the present discussion play a role in the disruption of the higher integrative functions. Geschwind and his colleagues[1] have extensively characterized the behavioral syndromes that result from focal damage to specific brain areas in terms of various combinations of functional loss and disconnection. For example, a patient with a stroke in a certain area of the left cerebral hemisphere who could both understand spoken language, and speak fluently and coherently, yet who could not repeat simple phrases spoken by the examiner, was thought to have suffered a disconnection between receptive and expressive language areas. Although not all of the neurobehavioral syndromes can be accounted for in terms of disconnection theory, it is not at all surprising that damage to one brain area may effectively disrupt the interconnections between other areas remote from the site of damage.

The results of such disconnections are rarely observed alone, however, since they are typically accompanied by the functional deficits resulting from the loss of the damaged area. In the preceding example, the stroke patient with poor repetition would probably also suffer from a word-finding problem and a mild decrease in comprehension because naturally occurring lesions such as stroke rarely produce highly circumscribed damage to specific cortical areas. To examine the effects of disconnection in relative isolation from other brain damage, one can look at cases of commissurotomy (the surgical separation of the cerebral hemispheres effected by cutting the corpus callosum). Before the effects of commissurotomy are considered, it would be useful first to review the functions of the cerebral hemispheres, and what interconnects them.

The Cerebral Hemispheres and the Corpus Callosum

One of the anchor points in contemporary thinking about how intellectual functions are represented in the brain is that language function is lateralized to the left cerebral hemisphere in most individuals. Since the early observations of Broca and Wernicke in the second half of the nineteenth century, it has been clearly demonstrated that in right-handed individuals, damage to the anterior half of the left hemisphere is associated with problems with the expression of language, whereas more posterior damage is associated with difficulties in language comprehension. Language problems, or aphasias, are usually independent of sensory modality, but specific syndromes may occur, where deficits can be selective, creating dysfunction in areas such as reading, writing, auditory comprehension or speech that are relatively more severe than those found for language function in general.

The lateralization of language functions to the left cerebral hemisphere is nearly universal in the right-handed population. In the left-handed population, lateralization of language is somewhat different. In addition to recording the incidence of aphasic disorders after unilateral brain damage in different subject groups, language lateralization can also be determined by a Wada test.[2] This procedure, which is typically performed after a cerebral arteriogram has been completed, involves injection of a barbiturate into the vascular distribution supplied by a carotid artery. The barbiturate typically produces a loss of function in the injected hemisphere for a period of approximately five minutes. During this time, the patient can be tested for the presence of aphasic symptoms. With the data obtained from a large series of Wada tests on left-handed patients, it has been estimated that approximately 70% of this group is left hemisphere dominant for language (like right-handers) and approximately 15% are right hemisphere dominant. The remaining 15% appear to have some degree of bilateral language representation.[3] Although there are still major questions to be answered about how language is organized in the brain, the effects of damage to language areas are clinically evident, and the strong association between expressive and receptive language and left hemisphere function is well accepted.

In contrast to what is known about cognitive function in the language hemisphere, function in the nonlanguage hemisphere is less well understood. The most frequently documented right hemisphere neurobehavioral syndrome is the so-called parietal-lobe syndrome. After damage to the nondominant parietal lobe, any or all of a number of disorders can be observed, each of which can be related to some aspect of appreciating spatial relationships, being able to direct one's attention in space, or being able to manipulate objects with some spatial reference. The patient with parietal lobe damage may exhibit a neglect phenomenon in which information appearing to the patient's left side (the side contralateral to the damage) is not acknowledged, and it is frequently impossible to have the patient orient into the impaired sensory hemifield. In extreme instances, patients may fail to dress the left side of their bodies, or deny that their left arm is their own. In less severe instances, patients may only lose information in the impaired sensory hemifield when information is also simultaneously presented to the intact sensory hemifield (extinction). Patients with parietal-lobe syndrome may also exhibit difficulties with spatial direction, repeatedly being unable to find their way back to their rooms, or with the manipulation of spatial relationships, having great difficulty copying geometric designs or reproducing constructions made of blocks or matchsticks.[4]

In addition to these largely visual, spatial functions, the nonlanguage hemisphere also demonstrates superiority in some auditory processes. This side of the brain has been regarded as playing an important role in the comprehension and expression of both music and emotion. Although it is an oversimplification to regard the nonlanguage hemisphere as dominant for either music[5] or emotion,[6] this side of the brain appears to play an important role in the appreciation of pitch, and may contribute to the control of vocal pitch in expression.[7] Thus, the comprehension and production of pitch information may be complementary in some ways to the language hemisphere's processing of speech information.

Between these functionally dissimilar hemispheres lies the corpus callosum, the largest fiber tract in the nervous system. Parts of the callosum project between visual, auditory, somatosensory, and motor areas in the two hemispheres, and it is now known that the callosum plays an important role in the transfer of cognitive as well as sensory information between the hemispheres.

The corpus callosum consists of a broad band of fibers that radiate into the white matter in both hemispheres. The midportion, or trunk, of the corpus callosum lies as a roof on the lateral ventricles. The anterior portion of the callosum curves downward and thins, becoming the genu and rostrum. At its posterior end, the corpus callosum becomes thickened and rounded at the splenium. Although this structure was first described by Galen (A.D. 131–201),[8] who believed that it played a role in suspending the hemispheres from the skull, the function of the corpus callosum in man has been established only during the past five decades. This understanding has come about through a combination of progress in animal experimentation, and the use of surgical excision of the corpus callosum in humans to aid in the control of otherwise intractable epilepsy.

A Paradox

The year 1940 was important in the contemporary study of the function of the corpus callosum. In that year, Erickson reported on his experimental work on the interhemispheric spread of epileptic activity in monkeys.[9] He concluded that the corpus callosum was responsible for the propagation of epileptic discharges from one hemisphere to another, and that surgically severing only part of the callosum was inadequate to prevent interhemispheric spread. In the same year, what is regarded as the first neurosurgical series of commissurotomy for epilepsy control was reported by Van Wagenen.[10]

The neurobehavioral consequences of commissurotomy in Van Wagenen's patients were studied by Akelaitis. It should be noted that Van Wagenen's patients were not all operated on in a similar manner: some underwent only partial commissurotomy, while some underwent commissurotomy in several stages. Moreover, Akelaitis was examining these patients in a fairly standard neurological fashion. At issue was the integrity of intellectual and motor functions, rather than the possibility that sensory systems might have been fragmented. A series of research reports[11] that began in 1941 focused on the surgery's effect on motor function and praxis, vision, color and object naming, reading and writing, and personality. Considering what was known about the very different functions of the two cerebral hemispheres, Akelaitis' conclusions that commissurotomy had little or no effect on the higher integrative functions presented a paradox. How could the surgical division of such functionally different brain structures produce so little behavioral change? Although in retrospect it is clear that Akelaitis' examinations revealed little about disconnection phenomena, the fact that the general behavior of commissurotomy patients is typically little changed by their surgery has been observed by every subsequent investigator.

Commissurotomy

Although Van Wagenen did not refer to Erickson's animal work when he presented his rationale for attempting to control seizures by commissurotomy,[12] subsequent animal work by Meyers and Sperry[13] explicitly provided some of the major steps in understanding the role of the corpus callosum in mediating the exchange of information between the hemispheres. After cutting the optic chiasm in cats, information could be presented to a single hemisphere by stimulating only one eye. Although animals trained on a discrimination task in this fashion could perform the learned discrimination with either the trained or untrained eye when the corpus callosum was intact, Meyers and Sperry demonstrated that the training was not available to both hemispheres when the corpus callosum was cut. This, and subsequent work, was important in demonstrating the role of the corpus callosum in the exchange of visual information between the hemispheres. Moreover, the insights gained in these animal studies played a key role in demonstrating the "split-brain" phenomenon in humans.

Commissurotomy for the control of epilepsy was once again undertaken in 1962 by Bogen and Vogel.[14] Their patients were initially studied by Gazzaniga and Sperry,[15] who described the disconnection syndrome produced by the surgery. Unlike the examinations performed by Akelaitis, the testing procedures were directed at disconnection and modified so that information was lateralized to a single hemisphere, visual guidance of motor acts was eliminated when inappropriate, and the opportunities for cross-cuing were restricted. Not only was it found that, after cutting the corpus callosum, information presented to one hemisphere was not available to the other hemisphere, but more significantly, in some cases each separated hemisphere could perceive and act on information out of conscious awareness of the other.[16] As the initial reports of the effects of commissurotomy were being provided by Gazzaniga and Sperry, Geschwind also began to formulate a disconnection theory based on observations of patients with focal neurological damage.[1] Similarly, studies from the Montreal Neurological Institute were focusing on hemispheric differences, largely in patients who were undergoing temporal lobectomy in an effort to control seizures.[17] The efforts of these different groups marked the beginning of a renewed interest in the functional differences between the two cerebral hemispheres.

The next development in human commissurotomy emerged with the Dartmouth series, begun by Wilson.[18] Wilson reviewed the work of Van Wagenen, Bogen, Luessenhop[19] and others, and judged that commissurotomy was effective in controlling seizures, and that it could be made safer with the use of microsurgical techniques. Wilson's procedure required less retraction of the brain during surgery, and he avoided entering the ventricles. As his surgical series grew, Wilson made several modifications to his technique, and eventually began to perform the complete commissurotomy in two stages: either the anterior or posterior half of the callosum would be sectioned in the first operation, with the remaining half sectioned in a second operation. Although the two-step commissurotomy was done for technical reasons, it provided the opportunity to study the function of the corpus callosum in more detail than had been possible when the entire callosum was sectioned in a single surgical session.

Sensory and Cognitive Disconnection

In humans, sensory systems and motor control are organized in what is essentially a contralateral fashion. In vision, for example, each hemisphere receives direct sensory information only from its contralateral field. Information in the ipsilateral visual field is provided by the corpus callosum, from the direct sensory input to the opposite hemisphere. Although the organization in other systems, like audition, is not as strictly contralateral, experimental control of stimulus conditions can be used to produce a situation much like that found in vision.

Some of the important properties of the corpus callosum as a sensory window between the hemispheres have been observed not only in patients who have undergone commissurotomy, but also in patients for whom the corpus callosum was damaged by vascular accident, tumor, or the need to penetrate the callosum surgically to approach another structure. Neuropsychological data obtained from these patient groups revealed that the posterior portion of the corpus callosum acts as a sensory window through which information about a hemisphere's ipsilateral sensory field is transferred. The splenium, which is at the most posterior extent of the callosum, mediates the exchange of visual information between the hemispheres.[20] Anterior to the splenium, but within the posterior half, are the areas responsible for the interhemispheric exchange of audition, touch, and motor control.[21] Cutting the posterior half of the corpus callosum, then, produces significant sensory disconnection, resulting in a patient who can look completely commissurotomized. This effect, and one of the strategies used to assess it, can be reviewed by referring to some data obtained from the first patient who underwent the staged surgical procedure in the Dartmouth series, patient J.W.

At the time of surgery, J.W. was a 24-year-old, right-handed man who had suffered from intractable epilepsy for seven years. He had been the product of a full term pregnancy and uncomplicated delivery, and he had reached the major psychomotor milestones normally. After concussive head trauma without skull fracture at age 13, J.W. began to experience infrequent episodes of absence spells. There were no tonic/clonic movements or other unusual behavior noted with these spells, and they were not treated. He graduated from high school at age 18, and one year later he experienced a major motor seizure. The subsequent neurological examination was normal, but an EEG revealed irregular polyspike and high-voltage repetitive 3-cps spike and wave bursts during sleep. The EEG abnormalities had a right anterior temporal prominence. Over the next seven years, he had multiple hospitalizations during which attempts were made to manage his epilepsy, which increased in severity. Neuropsychological assessment was carried out several days prior to J.W.'s posterior commissurotomy, and was repeated at intervals prior to and after completion of the commissurotomy.[22]

Tests of disconnection depend on the ability to present information to a single hemisphere. In vision, this means that the subject is required to maintain fixation on a central point. Stimuli are then briefly presented several degrees to the left or right of the central fixation. The brief presentation insures that the subject will not have sufficient time to make an eye movement to the stimulus while it is on the screen. Since the visual system is organized in a contralateral fashion, stimuli presented to the right of central fixation will be lateralized to the left hemisphere, stimuli presented to the left of central fixation will be lateralized to the right hemisphere. In audition, different stimuli must be simultaneously presented to each ear in close acoustic competition. When this dichotic mode of presentation is used appropriately, stimuli presented to the right ear are lateralized to the left hemisphere, while left ear stimuli are lateralized to the right hemisphere. Tactile stimulation is simply presented to one hand or the other, outside of vision, and

Table 6.1 Naming Accuracy (percent correct responses) on Stimuli Presented to the Left and Right Sensory Fields Prior to and Following Surgical Section of the Posterior Half of the Corpus Callosum

	Callosum Intact		Posterior Callosum Sectioned	
Modality	Left Sensory Field	Right Sensory Field	Left Sensory Field	Right Sensory Field
Vision				
Pictures	93	93	28	91
Words	63	92	13	96
Tactile				
Objects	100	100	20	90
Audition				
Speech Syllables	67	77	23	100

as in vision and audition, the lateralization of information is to the contralateral hemisphere.

In normal subjects, such lateralization procedures can produce perceptual asymmetries (e.g., a right ear advantage for speech discrimination) that reflect hemispheric differences (e.g., left hemisphere language dominance), but because the callosum is intact, such perceptual asymmetries are typically small, of the order of a 10% differential in performance between the two sensory fields. After commissurotomy, the situation is quite different.

Table 6.1 presents neuropsychological data obtained from J.W. before and after section of the posterior half of the corpus callosum. In addition to using the previously described techniques for lateralizing information to a single hemisphere, these particular tests also take advantage of the fact that the capacity for speech is lateralized to the left hemisphere in this patient. Unilateral speech makes testing for gross disconnection effects quite simple: If the callosum is intact, information presented to either hemisphere can be reported by the subject. However, if interhemispheric disconnection is present, then the subject will be able to report only information lateralized to the language hemisphere.

With the callosum intact, J.W.'s ability to name stimuli in either visual field was good. The right sensory field advantages for speech discrimination and reading are typically found in normal subjects, reflecting a left hemisphere language dominance. After the posterior portion of the corpus callosum was severed, several things occurred. In vision, touch, and audition, the ability to name stimuli presented to the left sensory field fell to chance. For vision and touch, the ability to name right field stimuli remained unchanged. For audition, performance on right ear stimuli actually improved. This reflects a release from competition in the dichotic procedure, which requires the simultaneous presentation of two different stimuli. Without the posterior callosum, the left ear stimulus is no longer transferred between hemispheres to compete with the right ear stimulus for left hemisphere processing.

If J.W.'s inability to name stimuli presented to the left sensory field is to be interpreted simply in terms of disconnection, it must also be shown that stimuli lateralized to the right hemisphere are being processed even though they cannot be named. A second phase of the neuropsychological assessment demonstrated that although stimuli lateralized to the right hemisphere could not be transferred to the left hemisphere for naming, they were being correctly interpreted within the right hemisphere. When J.W. was asked to respond by pointing with his left hand rather than by naming, the right hemisphere was 92% accurate at indicating picture-word correspondence for left visual field stimuli. This result not only indicated intact function in the right hemisphere, but also strongly suggested that J.W. could be included in the subset of commissurotomy patients with some capacity for language comprehension in the right hemisphere.

Although J.W.'s naming performance after only posterior callosal section was essentially identical to that found after complete commissurotomy, his verbal responses after right hemisphere stimulation were unlike those of a complete "split-brain" patient. Whereas such patients typically deny having seen anything after left visual field stimulation, J.W. did not. Instead, his failure to name stimuli lateralized to the right hemisphere was accompanied by apologies for a poor memory, and on occasion, a mildly agitated state like that described in the tip-of-the-tongue phenomenon.[23] On these occasions, the patient claimed to "see" the stimulus in his mind, but was unable to name or describe it.

After several such episodes, a game of "20 questions" was initiated with the patient whenever he felt that he had some sense of the information presented to the left visual field. This interaction would begin with the question, "Is it an object or a living thing?" and would include questions about form (e.g., large or small), function (e.g., used indoors or outdoors), and class (e.g., furniture or clothing). The 20-question interaction did not always result in J.W. being able to name the stimulus lateralized to his right hemisphere, but it was required for correct naming of such stimuli during the first two interoperative sessions. On one occasion, a drawing of a hunter's cap lateralized to the right hemisphere produced a strong sense of knowing without being able to name. After indicating in the 20-question interaction that the stimulus represented an object, J.W. rejected a number of object classes such as vehicle, tools, and housewares, until clothing was offered. He was then able to recognize the sex of the usual wearer, the season in which it is worn, and its typical color before finally naming the stimulus correctly.

Left visual field performance on picture- and word-naming tests administered before and after complete commissurotomy, and at intervals between the first (posterior section) and second stage (anterior section) surgeries are presented in Table 6.2. At each session, right visual field naming was highly accurate (greater than 90%). During the first interoperative session, left visual field word naming was at chance, but picture naming in that field was slightly, but significantly better than chance by virtue of the 20-question interaction. Throughout the interoperative period, J.W.'s left visual field naming improved, and by the seventh interoperative week (session three) he had adopted a self-generated inferential strategy based on his description of a mental image. For example, the word *stove* elicited descriptions of a country hardware store with a wood-burning stove, and an aunt's kitchen, with the latter description leading to the correct response. On another trial, the word *onion* elicited a description of the family garden. J.W. described these experiences as follows: "It's like things are moving around constantly, and I'm trying to narrow it down to something that will just stop. I'm seeing a whole general picture but one thing is almost right in the middle."

Table 6.2 J.W.'s Left Visual Field Performance (percent correct responses) on Picture- and Word-Naming Tests Administered at Each Operative Stage

	Stimuli	
Stage	*Pictures*	*Words*
Preoperative (8 August 1979)	93	63
Interoperative I* (24 August 1979)	28	13*
Interoperative II (15 September 1979)	67	42
Interoperative III (27 September 1979)	83	58
Postoperative (9 November 1979)	20†	0*

*The interoperative period refers to the interval following section of the posterior callosum but preceding complete section, which is represented at the postoperative stage. The initial surgery was performed on 10 August 1979, and the section was completed on 16 October 1979.
†Not significantly better than chance.

Although the transferred information was described in pictorial terms, the initial description was rarely that of the stimulus itself, but more likely of a context in which it might be found, or of some associate of the stimulus. Moreover, the transferred information was specific enough to avoid synonymous substitution errors (e.g., inferring that the original stimulus was the word *cap* rather than the word *hat,* that *auto* was *car,* or *boat* was *ship*), which might be expected if only referential "pictures" were being transferred. Homophonic errors were also largely avoided after left visual field stimulation (75% accuracy). Of the four errors made on this test, two were unrelated to the original stimuli, and two consisted of the incorrect spellings (i.e., *tail* for *tale*) although in one of these, subsequent usage indicated that the correct meaning had been preserved. There were no errors on right visual field homophones.

The inference process used by J.W. was not always lengthy, nor was it always vocalized. Even in the tenth interoperative week, however, the naming of left visual field was rarely immediate, occurring quickly only for stimuli associated with some strong personal interest (such as *car*). After the callosum was completely sectioned, left visual field naming did not differ significantly from chance. J.W. no longer attempted the inference strategy, and as with other complete "split-brain" patients, he then denied any experience following left visual field stimulation. Figure 6.1 depicts a schematic representation of J.W.'s naming ability for left visual field stimuli at each operative stage.

These observations demonstrated that the corpus callosum plays an important role in interhemispheric communication at several levels. It provides visual, auditory, and somatosensory information from the ipsilateral sensory field. It mediates ipsilateral motor control of the distal extremities. In addition to this sensory and motor transfer, the anterior portion of this tract provides higher-order information, transferring the results of cognitive processing in each hemisphere. The cognitive interactions between J.W.'s hemispheres were based on stimulus-related semantic and episodic information. After right visual field stimulation in the interoperative period, the expressive language system lateralized to the left hemisphere had direct access to both the sensory and higher-order information retrieved from memory. After left visual field stimulation in the interoperative period, however, there was no sensory transfer from the right hemisphere to the expressive language

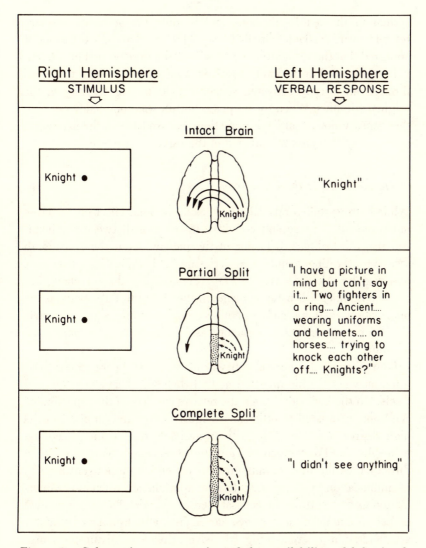

Figure 6.1 Schematic representation of the availability of left visual field stimuli for naming by the left hemisphere at each operative stage.

system in the left hemisphere, and so only the activated memory referents were available initially for verbal report. On those occasions, it appeared that the recognition process occurred in reverse. The inferential process used in the interoperative period seemed to reflect a search through an already activated semantic field for the identity of the original stimulus. When the corpus callosum was completely cut, neither sensory nor cognitive information was available to the expressive language system after stimulation of the right hemisphere.

Some Answers to the Paradox

While cutting the corpus callosum has a profound effect on the cross integration of sensory and cognitive information between the hemispheres, the ordinary behavior of the patients from the Dartmouth series and the Bogen and Vogel series probably differs little from that observed by Akelaitis years earlier. Personalities do not change or become fragmented, patients maintain the ability to talk about spatial information, their speech does not become monotonic, and they generally do not report much difficulty associated with their perceptual disconnection.

How, then, is this normal behavior maintained? There appear to be some answers to this question at both behavioral and physiological levels. On the behavioral level, the relative subtlety of the "split-brain" syndrome compared to other neurological syndromes emphasizes the high degree of behavioral plasticity available to two intact cerebral hemispheres. To compensate for the absence of information flow through the callosum, commissurotomy patients attempt to ensure such communication by using any information available. Much of the information lost by cutting the callosal "sensory window" can be provided by behavioral means such as eye movements, visual guidance of motor acts, and auditory cross-cuing. Moreover, since commissurotomy produces no apparent loss of specific cognitive function in either hemisphere, the subject has two brain systems contributing to the behavioral compensation for disconnection, without having to compensate additionally for gaps in cognitive function. The grossly normal behavior of commissurotomy patients, then, demonstrates the competence of intact cognitive systems in using neural, perceptual, and behavioral information to integrate left and right hemisphere functions in the absence of the corpus callosum. It also demonstrates a strong drive toward unified behavior.

Apart from the behavioral strategies these patients use to integrate the information available to each hemisphere, there also appear to be other more subtle forms of interhemispheric interaction that occur without the corpus callosum or behavioral strategy, which provide some of the threads that bind the experiences of the two hemispheres to a single person. One such interaction occurs in the presence of bilateral language function.[24]

It was suggested in a previous section that in some commissurotomy patients, although the left hemisphere is dominant for language, there is also some capacity in the right hemisphere for language comprehension. This is not present in all patients, and its extent is quite variable among those patients who have it.[25] J.W. is one such patient, however, and he has demonstrated a subtle, but significant form of semantic interaction between the hemispheres without a corpus callosum.

Reconsidering the cognitive interactions between the hemispheres that were observed in J.W. after he had only the posterior portion of the callosum sectioned, one of the implications of those results was that the two hemispheres represented cognitive information in very similar ways. Had the two hemispheres been operating with very different cognitive "styles" or had their linguistic representations been qualitatively different, J.W.'s inferential strategy would probably have been useless. That was not the case, and subsequent work on the ability of each hemisphere to make semantic judgments after complete commissurotomy revealed similar patterns for the two hemispheres.[25] That work, together with the interoperative cognitive interactions observed in J.W., suggested the possibility that each hemisphere accessed a functionally common semantic system. Although overt interhemispheric interactions no longer occurred after complete commissurotomy, the possibility that a more subtle form of interaction could occur was examined by using the phenomenon known as semantic priming.

In the normal subjects, it can be shown that reading a word leaves a residual effect that can influence the processing of subsequent words. For example, semantic relatedness among a group of words can significantly facilitate word/nonword judgments[26] or semantic category judgments[27] of those words. The facilitation, or priming effect, reflects both the structure of the semantic system and the process by which it is activated. A semantic priming paradigm was used with J.W. to address two questions. First, would the language capacities represented in each hemisphere benefit from processing semantically related items? This question addresses possible left/right differences in semantic information processing in the two hemispheres. The second question is more relevant for the issue of disconnection: If semantic priming effects occurred within each hemisphere, could priming also be observed across hemispheres? This second question addresses the degree to which semantic processing occurs independently in each hemisphere.

Figure 6.2 depicts a semantic relationship between words for both within- and between-hemisphere conditions. After the presentation of each word, the patient was asked to classify it as referring to something artificial or something natural by manually pressing one of two keys. Four conditions were tested in each hemisphere. Target words were preceded by either an unrelated word in the same category (e.g., *ship—*

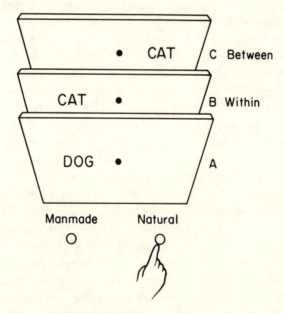

Figure 6.2 Typical within-hemisphere and between-hemisphere semantically related trials in the priming study. (Accuracy and latency scores were obtained from performance on the word following the priming word, although the patient responded to every word.)

gate), or a related word in the same category (e.g., *ship–boat*), and the preceding word appeared in either the same visual field as the target (the within-hemisphere condition) or in the visual field opposite that in which the target appeared (the between-hemisphere condition).

Some of the results of this study are presented in table 6.3.[28] There was a significant facilitation due to semantic relatedness in both the within- and between-hemisphere conditions. These results provide additional evidence indicating that the semantic representations available to the left and right hemispheres of a bilaterally represented language system are processed in a qualitatively similar manner. More important to the present discussion, however, is the observation that the semantic processing that occurs in one hemisphere of a bilateral language system is not independent of semantic processing that occurs in the other hemisphere, even after complete section of the corpus callosum. It appears, then, that both sides of a bilaterally represented language system maintain access to a functionally common semantic system.

Although the completely commissurotomized patient cannot verbally report information presented to the right hemisphere, such information may nevertheless have a subtle influence on information processing in the left hemisphere. The commissurotomy patient's behavioral attempts

Table 6.3 Accuracy and Latency of Semantic Categorization Judgments

	Left Hemisphere		Right Hemisphere	
	Preceding Word Semantically		Preceding Word Semantically	
Condition	Related	Unrelated	Related	Unrelated
Accuracy (percent correct)				
Within-hemisphere	92.6	79.5	82.1	60.9
Between-hemisphere	92.0	82.9	88.5	58.3
Latency (msec)*				
Within-hemisphere	1,390(64)	1,469(65)	1,142(62)	1,493(66)
Between-hemisphere	1,427(76)	1,604(68)	1,385(77)	1,723(79)

*The standard errors of the means are given in parentheses.

at compensating for disconnection may well be influenced by semantic and spatial information that is unavailable for verbal report.

Disconnection and Dissociation

The paradoxical absence of striking changes in general behavior after commissurotomy stands as a counterpoint to dissociative phenomena. After "splitting" the brain, sensory function, perception, and even cognition can be fragmented, but to our eyes and to any ordinary definition of personality, the person remains. But more than that, the person who remains adapts to disconnection, in some ways that are behaviorally obvious, such as cross-cuing, and in other ways that we are just beginning to observe, such as by making use of semantic and spatial information that is not readily available for conscious processing.

Disconnection, then, does not provide a model for dissociative phenomena. On the contrary, one could use the example of the "split-brain" as evidence of the strength of the drive toward a unified functional state. The observations that, when surgically separated, the two cerebral hemispheres can subserve relatively independent cognitive function and that, in some psychiatric conditions, people can experience dissociative phenomena, can presently be viewed as no more than examples of functional uncouplings from which some interesting parallels may be drawn. This is not to say that the cerebral hemispheres have no role in dissociative phenomena, but rather that such phenomena represent a process far more complicated than simple disconnection.

References and Notes

1. N. Geschwind and E. Kaplan, "A Human Cerebral Disconnection Syndrome," *Neurology* 12 (1962): 675–685; N. Geschwind, "Disconnection Syndromes in Animals and Man. Part I," *Brain* 88 (1965a): 237–294; N. Geschwind, "Disconnection Syndromes in Animals and Man. Part II," *Brain* 88 (1965b): 595–644; and N. Geschwind, F. A. Quadfasel, and J. M. Segarra, "Isolation of the Speech Area," *Neuropsychologia* 6 (1968): 327–340.
2. J. Wada and T. Rasmussen, "Intracarotid Injection of Sodium Amytal for the Lateralization of Cerebral Speech Dominance," *Journal of Neurosurgery* 17 (1960): 266–282; and E. A. Serafetinides, R. D. Hoare, and M. V. Driver, "Intracarotid Sodium Amylobarbitone and Cerebral Dominance for Speech and Consciousness," *Brain* 88 (1965): 107–130.

3. C. Branch, B. Milner, and T. Rasmussen, "Intracarotid Sodium Amytal for the Lateralization of Cerebral Speech Dominance: Observations on 123 Patients," *Journal of Neurosurgery* 21 (1964): 399–405; and T. Rasmussen and B. Milner, "The Role of Early Left-Brain Injury in Determining Lateralization of Cerebral Speech Functions," *Annals of the New York Academy of Sciences* 299 (1977): 355–369.
4. For a review, see E. DeRenzi, *Disorders of Space Exploration and Cognition*. New York: Wiley, 1982.
5. A. Gates, and J. L. Bradshaw, "The Role of the Cerebral Hemispheres in Music," *Brain and Language* 4 (1977): 403–431; and J. C. M. Brust, "Music and Language: Musical Alexia and Agraphia," *Brain* 103 (1980): 367–392.
6. J. T. Cacioppo, R. E. Petty, and C. W. Snyder, "Cognitive and Affective Response as a Function of Relative Hemispheric Involvement," *International Journal of Neuroscience* 9 (1979): 81–89; G. Gainotti, "Affectivity and Brain Dominance: A Survey," in J. Obiols, C. Ballus, E. Gonzales Monclus, and J. Pujol, eds., *Biological Psychiatry Today*. Amsterdam: Elsevier/North-Holland Biomedical Press, 1979; and R. G. Ley and M. P. Bryden, "The Right Hemisphere and Emotion," in G. Underwood and R. Stevens, eds., *Aspects of Consciousness*, vol. 2. New York: Academic Press, 1981.
7. J. J. Sidtis, "Music, Pitch Perception, and the Mechanisms of Cortical Hearing," in M. S. Gazzaniga, ed., *Handbook of Cognitive Neuroscience*. New York: Plenum Press, 1984.
8. Galen (c. A.D. 131–201) cited by F. N. L. Poynter, *The Brain and Its Functions*. Oxford: Blackwell, 1957; and W. J. K. Cumming, "An Anatomical Review of the Corpus Callosum," *Cortex* 6 (1970): 1–8.
9. T. C. Erickson, "Spread of Epileptic Discharge," *Archives of Neurology* 43 (1940): 429–452.
10. W. P. Van Wagenen and R. Y. Herren, "Surgical Division of Commissural Pathways in the Corpus Callosum," *Archives of Neurology* 44 (1940): 740–759.
11. A. J. Akelaitis, "Psychobiological Studies following Section of the Corpus Callosum," *American Journal of Psychiatry* 97 (1941a): 1147–1157; A. J. Akelaitis, "Studies on the Corpus Callosum. VIII. The Effects of Partial and Complete Section of the Corpus Callosum on Psychopathic Epileptics," *American Journal of Psychiatry* 98 (1941b): 409–414; A. J. Akelaitis, "Studies on the Corpus Callosum. II. The Higher Visual Functions in Each Homonymous Field following Complete Section of the Corpus Callosum," *Archives of Neurological Psychiatry* 45 (1941c): 788–796; A. J. Akelaitis, "Studies on the Corpus Callosum. VII. Study of Language Functions (Tactile and Visual Lexia and Graphia) Unilaterally following Section of the Corpus Callosum," *Journal of Neuropathology and Experimental Neurology* 2 (1943): 226–262; and A. J. Akelaitis, "Study on

Gnosia, Praxia, and Language following Section of Corpus Callosum and Anterior Commissure," *Journal of Neurosurgery* 1 (1944): 94–102.

12. D. H. Wilson, A. Reeves, and M. S. Gazzaniga, "Corpus Callosotomy for Control of Intractable Seizures," in J. A. Wada and J. K. Penry, eds., *Advances in Epileptology*. New York: Raven Press, 1980.

13. R. E. Meyers and R. W. Sperry, "Interocular Transfer of a Visual Form Discrimination Habit in Cats after Section of the Optic Chiasma and Corpus Callosum," *Anatomical Record* 115 (1953): 351–352; R. E. Meyers, "Function of the Corpus Callosum in Interocular Transfer," *Brain* 79 (1956): 358–363; and R. E. Meyers, "Transmission of Visual Information within and between the Hemispheres," in V. B. Mountcastle, ed., *Interhemispheric Relations and Cerebral Dominance*. Baltimore: Johns Hopkins University Press, 1962.

14. J. E. Bogen and P. J. Vogel, "Cerebral Commissurotomy in Man," *Bulletin of the Los Angeles Neurological Society* 27 (1965): 169–174.

15. M. S. Gazzaniga, *The Bisected Brain*. New York: Appleton-Century-Crofts, 1970; M. S. Gazzaniga, J. E. Bogen, and R. W. Sperry, "Some Functional Effects of Sectioning the Cerebral Commissures in Man," *Proceedings of the National Academy of Sciences* 48 (1962): 1765–1769; M. S. Gazzaniga and J. E. LeDoux, *The Integrated Mind*. New York: Plenum Press, 1978; M. S. Gazzaniga and R. W. Sperry, "Language after Section of the Cerebral Commissures," *Brain* 90 (1967): 131–148; and R. W. Sperry, M. S. Gazzaniga, and J. E. Bogen, "Interhemispheric Relationships: The Neocortical Commissures, Syndromes of Hemispheric Disconnection," in P. J. Vinken and G. W. Bruyn, eds., *Handbook of Clinical Neurology*, vol. 4. *Disorders of Speech, Perception and Symbolic Behavior*. Amsterdam: Elsevier/North-Holland Biomedical Press, 1969.

16. The issue of consciousness after commissurotomy is extensively reviewed in a monograph by C. E. Marks, *Commissurotomy, Consciousness and Unity of Mind*. Montgomery, Vt.: Bradford, 1980.

Also see: R. W. Sperry, "Hemispheric Deconnection and Unity in Conscious Awareness," *American Psychologist* 23 (1968): 723–733; M. S. Gazzaniga, "One Brain—Two Minds," *American Scientist* 60 (1972): 311–317; and D. M. MacKay, "Cerebral Organization and the Conscious Control of Action," in J. C. Eccles, ed., *Brain and Conscious Experience*. Heidelberg: Springer, 1966.

17. B. Milner, "Laterality Effects in Audition," in V. B. Mountcastle, ed., *Interhemispheric Relations and Cerebral Dominance*. Baltimore: Johns Hopkins University Press, 1962; and Wada and Rasmussen "Intracarotid Injection," (1960), note 2.

18. D. H. Wilson, C. Culver, M. Waddington, and M. S. Gazzaniga, "Disconnection of the Cerebral Hemispheres," *Neurology* 25 (1975): 1149–1153; and D. H. Wilson, A. Reeves, and M. S. Gazzaniga, "Division of the Corpus Callosum for Uncontrollable Epilepsy," *Neurology* 28 (1978): 649–653.

19. A. J. Luessenhop, T. C. Delacruz, and G. M. Fenichel, "Surgical Discon-
    nection of the Cerebral Hemispheres for Intractable Seizures," *Journal of
    the American Medical Association* 213 (1970): 1630–1636.
20. J. H. Trescher and F. R. Ford, "Colloid Cyst of the Third Ventricle,"
    Archives of Neurology and Psychiatry 37 (1937): 959–964; P. E. Maspes,
    "Le syndrome expérimental chez l'homme de la section du splénium du
    corps calleux alexie visuelle pure hémianopsique," *Revue Neurologique* 80
    (1948): 100–113; M. S. Gazzaniga and H. Freedman, "Observations on
    Visual Process after Posterior Callosal Section," *Neurology* 23 (1973):
    1126–1130; and M. Sugishita, M. Iwata, Y. Toyokura, M. Yoshioko, and
    R. Yamada, "Reading of Ideograms and Phonograms in Japanese follow-
    ing Partial Commissurotomy," *Neuropsychologia* 16 (1978): 417–425.
21. J. J. Sidtis, B. T. Volpe, J. D. Holtzman, D. H. Wilson, and M. S.
    Gazzaniga, "Cognitive Interaction after Staged Callosal Section: Evidence
    for Transfer of Semantic Activation," *Science* 212 (1981a): 344–346;
    S. P. Springer and M. S. Gazzaniga, "Dichotic Testing of Partial and
    Complete Split-Brain Subjects," *Neuropsychologia* 13 (1975): 341–346;
    and B. T. Volpe, J. J. Sidtis, J. D. Holtzman, D. H. Wilson, and M. S.
    Gazzaniga, "Cortical Mechanisms Involved in Praxis: Observations Fol-
    lowing Partial and Complete Section of the Corpus Callosum," *Neurology*
    32 (1982): 645–650.
22. J. J. Sidtis, et al., "Cognitive Interaction," (1981a), note 21.
23. R. Brown, and D. McNeill, "The Tip-of-the-Tongue Phenomenon," *Jour-
    nal of Verbal Learning and Verbal Behavior* 5 (1966): 325–336.
24. Interhemispheric interactions have been observed for the control of atten-
    tion and the allocation of resources after complete section of the corpus
    callosum. See J. D. Holtzman, J. J. Sidtis, B. T. Volpe, D. H. Wilson,
    and M. S. Gazzaniga, "Dissociation of Spatial Information for Stimulus
    Localization and the Control of Attention," *Brain* 104 (1981): 861–872;
    and J. D. Holtzman and M. S. Gazzaniga, "Dual Task Interactions Due
    Exclusively to Limits in Processing Resources," *Science* 218 (1982):
    1325–1327.
25. J. J. Sidtis, B. T. Volpe, M. Rayport, D. H. Wilson, and M. S. Gazzaniga,
    "Variability in Right Hemisphere Language Function after Callosal Sec-
    tion: Evidence for a Continuum of Generative Capacity," *Journal of Neu-
    roscience* 1 (1981b): 323–331.
26. D. E. Meyer and R. W. Schvaneveldt, "Meaning, Memory Structure and
    Mental Processes," *Science* 192 (1976): 27–33.
27. F. T. Durso and M. K. Johnson, "Facilitation in Naming and Categoriz-
    ing Repeated Pictures and Words," *Journal of Experimental Psychology:
    Human Learning and Memory* 5 (1979): 449–459.
28. J. J. Sidtis, "Bilateral Language and Commissurotomy: Interactions be-
    tween the Hemispheres with and without the Corpus Callosum," in A.
    Reeves, ed., *Epilepsy and the Corpus Callosum*. New York: Plenum Press,
    1985.

7. Horror and Dissociation with Examples from Edgar Allan Poe

George Stade, Ph.D.

The first whodunnit ever written, "The Murders in the Rue Morgue," begins as though it were an essay—or more accurately, as though it were a paper to be read before a gathering of psychical researchers. A peculiarly emphatic speaker, who never identifies himself, is going on about something he calls *analysis*. "The mental features discoursed of as the analytical," he says, "are, in themselves, but little susceptible of analysis. We appreciate them only in their effects." We do know, our speaker continues, that the possessor of analytic powers derives from them "the liveliest enjoyment." He therefore searches out enigmas of all kinds—and solves them, too. His solutions seem "preternatural" to the layman; they have about them "the whole air of intuition," or worse, improvisation; but in fact they are achieved "by the very soul and essence of method." His method, however, is not that of the master chess player or mathematician, mere calculators whose reputations for analytic prowess are very much exaggerated. No, the true analyst is imaginative rather than ingenious—and that is why he alone excels in "these more important undertakings where mind struggles with mind." His method is nothing less than identification: "Deprived of ordinary resources, the analyst throws himself into the spirit" of the mind he is trying to master "and identifies himself therewith."

Just as we are beginning to wonder whether Edgar Allan Poe, in 1841, wrote an anticipatory apology for psychoanalysis, the essay turns into a story. Abruptly, we are introduced to an extraordinary friend of the narrator's, a certain C. Auguste Dupin. They met, characteristically enough, in an obscure library, both of them "in search of the same very rare and remarkable volume," for they are alike in valuing only those things that the world despises. Dupin, we read, is a ruined aristocrat who has "ceased to bestir himself in the world, or to care for the retrieval of his fortunes"—he is the very antithesis of the bustling burgher, the Western world's new exemplary man, his tastes the latest thing, his standards the grounds for invidious comparisons with everything else. Dupin's aesthetic withdrawal and aristocratic disdain attract him to the narrator, as "the wild fervor, and the vivid freshness of his imagination." At the narrator's expense they set up housekeeping together in a "time-eaten and grotesque mansion, long deserted through superstitions . . . in a retired and desolate portion of the Faubourg St. Germain." They furnish this atmospheric pile, according to the narrator, in a style that "suited the fantastic gloom of our common temper."

Each morning at first dawn, they shut out the daylight with "mossy shutters," ignite a couple of feeble and perfumed candles, and mope around dreaming, reading, writing, and talking. "We existed within ourselves alone," says the narrator. At night they wander arm in arm through "the wild lights and shadows of the populous city." Had their routine become known, our narrator boasts, "we should have been regarded as madmen." During one of their nocturnal excursions, Dupin demonstrates his uncanny powers as an analyst. He uncoils the chain of associations, of many tangled links, that flitted through the narrator's mind from the time a fruiterer bumped into him until, minutes later, he glanced up at the constellation of Orion. And the whole passage reads like something that Freud, perhaps wisely, cut out of *The Interpretation of Dreams*. The narrator, acting for the first time like his descendant, Dr. Watson, is astounded. With respect to himself, observes Dupin, most men "wore windows in their bosoms." Here is how Dupin, when taken by a fit of analysis, looks to his sidekick:

His manner at these moments was frigid and abstract; his eyes were vacant in expression; while his voice, usually a rich tenor, rose into a treble which would have sounded petulantly but for the deliberateness and entire distinction of the enunciation. Observing him in these moods, I often dwelt meditatively upon the old philosophy of the Bi-Part Soul, and amused myself with the fancy of a double Dupin—the creative and the resolvent.

Just as we might expect, the first (psycho-) analyst had an unstable personality. And as we might have guessed, it is precisely when he undertakes an analysis that he dissociates, that an otherwise hidden self takes over, one whose manner is frigid and abstract, the eyes vacant, the voice pedantic. A marginal type to begin with, at odds with his time and place, out of touch with common humanity, an *artiste manqué* with scientific pretensions, gloomy, eccentric, fantastical, irresistibly drawn to the dark undersides of things, a kind of secular necromancer, Poe's analyst is good at sniffing out crime and madness because he has an affinity for them. In that respect nothing has changed. At least, I hope not. Poe's narrator, in any case, assures us that Dupin's strange manner when in an analytic mood is not some fantasy out of a romance, but "merely the result of an excited, or perhaps of a diseased intelligence."

What Poe depicted in Dupin's fit of analysis, of course, we now call "dissociation"; but what Poe himself thought he meant by "the old philosophy of the Bi-Part Soul" is another matter. His annotators are not of much help. Two of the most recent, summing up over a century of commentary, note that "no one seems able to explain exactly what Poe means by 'the old philosophy of the Bi-Part Soul.'"[1] Poe's own essays, letters, and marginalia are also of little help. None of them discuss the Bi-Part Soul. Neither do Poe's stories, although one of them besides "The Murders in the Rue Morgue" mentions it. What his stories do, rather, is depict bi-, tri-, and poly-part souls at all angles of attraction and repulsion to each other.

The other story that mentions the Bi-Part Soul is one of Poe's first, a spoof called "Lionizing." There we are introduced to a character called Aestheticus Ethix. "He spoke of fire, unity, and atoms; bi-part and pre-existent soul; affinity and discord; primitive intelligence and homo-omaria." That's all we hear about him, but what we do hear is enough to tell us that he is both ethical and aesthetical, traits normally opposed to each other, except in works of art; that in him discords have an affinity for each other; and that he is familiar with both primitive intelligence and homoomaria, which may be defined as "the doctrine that elementary substances are composed of parts each similar to the whole"[2]—a doctrine that applies both to works of art (in romantic theory) and selves composed of harmonious subselves.

In an ideally integrated self, that is, each subself is synecdochically related to the whole: each is identical to the whole, yet distinguishable from it, as in that other brainteaser, the dogma of the Trinity. But in Poe's horror stories, the self is full of flaws; along these it splits, fractures, and falls apart into independent agents that haunt, menace, and possess each other, unto madness or death. All that is what makes them horror stories. It is to them that I shall now detour in the hopes that we can return to "The Murders in the Rue Morgue" with a better sense of just what horror, what primitive intelligence it is that Dupin alone is able to identify, identify with, and exorcise through analysis.

The Poe story most discussed by students of dissociation and *Doppelgänger* is, of course, "William Wilson." William Wilson, who tells his own story, tells us early on that William Wilson is not his real name, which, however, is equally plebian, redundant, and detestable. He is a rich English commoner with aristocratic yearnings. He is also the product of an inherited hyperactive imagination and indulgent parents, who spoil him. By the time he is sent away to school, he is excitable, capricious, imperious, self-willed, malicious, and "prey to the most ungovernable passions"—in short, a brat. You would think, then, that he would blame his upbringing or himself for his grownup years of what he calls "unparalleled infamy" and "unpardonable crime." But he does not. Instead, he pleads with the reader to believe that in all his many crimes he has been "the slave of circumstances beyond human control." He does not, as would his modern equivalent, say that society made him do it, whatever the *it* might be. The something that made him do it, although outside his control, bears his name, was born on the same day, looks and dresses like him, and speaks with his voice, if only and always in *"a very low whisper."*

William Wilson first meets this "fatality," this other William Wilson at school, at an academy that quickly becomes a metaphor for the mind, for the mind as Poe understands it, which is pretty much how the more pessimistic and skeptical among us still understand it. The grounds of the academy are entirely enclosed by a high, wide brick wall, its top embedded with broken glass. The enclosed grounds are extensive— impossible to say how extensive, for they are irregular and full of out-of-the-way recesses. Even more impossible to survey is the gothic house in which the boys study and sleep:

There was really no end to its windings—to its incomprehensible subdivisions [says William Wilson]. It was difficult, at any given time, to say with certainty upon which of the two stories one happened to be. From each room to every other there were sure to be found three or four steps either in ascent or descent. Then the lateral branches were innumerable—inconceivable—and so returning in upon themselves, that our most exact ideas in regards to the whole mansion were not very far different from those with which we pondered upon infinity.

There are two stories, that's clear, a higher level and a lower, one resolvent and one creative perhaps, or one devoted to consciousness and rule and one given over to dreams and impulse. But from the inside you cannot tell which is which, and there is no other place but inside—a discouraging picture of the mind for anybody who hopes to learn about it through introspection or observation. The large schoolroom, magazine and dispensary of our culture's accrued learning, is equally a maze:

Interspersed about the room, crossing and recrossing in endless irregularity, were innumerable benches and desks, black, ancient, and time-worn, piled desperately with much bethumbed books, and so beseamed with initial letters, names at full length, grotesque figures, and other multiplied efforts of the knife, as to have entirely lost what little of original form might have been their portion in days long departed.

Amid the mind's cultural clutter, amid this imagery of the desperately piled and half-effaced detritus of humanity's attempts to understand or make its mark on the world, there is only one nook of order and certainty. "In a remote and terror-inspiring angle was a square enclosure of eight or ten feet, comprising the *sanctum* of the school's principal"—and a very neat image of what we now call the superego is this principal, who is also the school's pastor. Here is how he looks to William Wilson as he presides over the services to which the students are marched twice each Sunday:

With how deep a spirit of wonder and perplexity was I wont to regard him from our remote pew in the gallery, as, with a step solemn and slow, he ascended the pulpit! This reverent man, with countenance so demurely benign, with robes so glossy and so clerically flowing, with wig so minutely powdered, so rigid and so vast,—would this be he who, of late, with sour visage, and in snuffy habiliments, administered, ferule in hand, the Draconian laws of the academy? Oh, gigantic paradox, too utterly monstrous for solution!

Principal and pastor, benign and forbidding, enforcer of the tribe's secular precepts and religious values, the Reverend Dr. Bransby is the story's one distinct character. His indistinct proxy among the boys arrives on the same day as William Wilson. This second William Wilson becomes the first William Wilson's only rival for supremacy among the boys. He is the only boy, says the first William Wilson, "to refuse implicit belief in my assertions, and submission to my will—indeed to interfere with my arbitrary dictation in any respect whatsoever." The second William Wilson seems to exist only to "thwart, astonish, or mortify" his namesake; and what is particularly galling, he does it all with a "most unwelcome *affectionateness* of manner."

At the beginning, William Wilson cannot bring himself to hate his rival altogether. After all, imitation is a form of flattery. And there were "many strong points of congeniality" in their tempers. Further, the admonitions of his rival, says William Wilson, were always ethically sound—"his moral sense, at least, if not his general talents and worldly wisdom, was far keener than my own." The two become "the most inseparable of companions." But only for a while. Soon, the second William Wilson's "intolerable spirit of contradiction," his "distasteful supervision," his "disgusting air of patronage," turns the first William Wilson's tolerance into "positive hatred." Above all, he cannot bear the thought that someone might allude to a similarity between them, although no one does. He makes his feelings known. The second William Wilson shies away. With neurotic logic, the first William becomes all the more enraged.

One night, an unspecified mean trick in mind, he steals through "a wilderness of narrow passages," through "many little nooks or recesses, the odds and ends of the structure," in which the boys have their separate rooms, to his rival's chamber. He draws back the bed curtains and shines his lamp on the sleeper's face, which he seems now to see clearly for the first time. What follows is a classical description of someone in the throes of horror:

I looked;—and a numbness, an iciness of feeling instantly pervaded my frame. My breast heaved, my knees tottered, my whole spirit became possessed with an objectless yet intolerable horror. Gasping for breath, I lowered the lamp in still nearer proximity to the face. Were these—*these* the lineaments of William Wilson? I saw, indeed, that they were his, but I shook as if with a fit of ague in fancying they were not.

That's all we are told: the horror is intolerable, but objectless; the sleeper's face is familiar, yet strange—*heimlich* and *unheimlich*, we might say. That's all, but it is enough to make William Wilson flee the academy at once.

At Eton, William Wilson plunges into a "vortex of thoughtless folly," of "soulless dissipation" and novel "debaucheries." Once, at the climax of an all-night bash, "while our delirious extravagance was at its height," just as William Wilson is about to propose an especially profane toast, a visitor arrives. William Wilson meets him in the vestibule, in the dim light of which the stranger's features are obscured. The stranger merely seizes William Wilson by the arm, and in a familiar voice whispers their name in his ear. It's enough to send William Wilson packing—to Oxford, where he throws off all restraints "in the mad infatuation of his revels," as he puts it. Though already too rich for anybody's good, he stoops to cheating at cards. He can't say why, exactly—because of the enormity of the offense maybe, because it's the lowest crime he can think of, to vex himself, to thwart his namesake. But William Wilson's namesake is the kind of entity that thwarts you precisely and only when you try to evade him. One night, when William Wilson is on the verge of ruining "a young *parvenu* nobleman," all the doors of the gaming room suddenly fly open; the candles "as if by magic" go out; a figure whose presence can be felt but not seen tells everybody present how William Wilson has been playing with a marked deck; he then disappears. William Wilson, as you can well imagine, flees Oxford "in a perfect agony of horror and shame."

But he flees in vain. His "spectral" pursuer thwarts his ambition at Rome, his revenge at Paris, his passionate love at Naples, his schemes in Egypt, Vienna, Berlin, and Moscow. The climax is vintage Poe. It is carnival time in Rome. The Duke Di Broglio throws a masquerade ball in his mazy palazzo. The wine flows, especially into William Wilson, who has become something of a lush. The setting, recurrent in Poe's stories, is one of disinhibition: the costumes, the masks, the wine, the dancing and music melt character armor. William Wilson is looking for "the young, the gay, the beautiful wife of the aged and doting Di Broglio." He is arrested by a hand on his shoulder, a whisper in his ear, by a figure in a costume exactly like his own. He drags the figure into an antechamber, challenges him, draws, and as he says, "plunged my sword, with brute ferocity, repeatedly through and through his bosom."

Someone tries the latch on the door; William Wilson hurries off to prevent any intrusion—outside reality beckons, that is, but is sealed off. He returns: "what human language," he asks, "can adequately portray *that* astonishment, *that* horror which possessed me at the spectacle then presented to view?" The horror that possesses William Wilson is this: the whole further end of the room has turned into a mirror in which he sees himself, all over bloody, advancing to meet himself. But no, integration never occurs; the mirror image resolves itself into the other William Wilson, who speaks the story's final words:

'You have conquered, and I yield. Yet, henceforward art thou also dead—dead to the World, to Heaven, and to Hope! In me didst thou exist—and in my death, see by this image, which is thy own, how utterly thou has murdered thyself.'

These last words are spoken not in a whisper, but in a voice that William Wilson finally recognizes as his own. For the sake of the story, I wish that the two of them had for once kept their single mouth shut. What I mean is that those portentous last words nearly succeed in reducing the tale to an allegory. Taken allegorically, William Wilson becomes that portion of the self that is aware of itself, that wills and reflects, the ego, if you will. The Reverend Dr. Bransby, principal and pastor, then becomes the rules and values of William Wilson's culture, as far as they have been internalized. The school and its grounds would represent the rest of the mind and its contents; the other characters would represent internalized public opinion. And the whole story becomes a cautionary tale in the usual tautological manner: if you kill your conscience, it will die; crime and vice are their own punishment, as all sinners, to their sorrow, will ultimately learn.

But somehow "William Wilson" does not feel like a cautionary tale; it feels like a horror story. After any allegorical reading of it, something is left over, and that something is horror, the subject to which I shall now turn. Having detoured from my account of "The Murders in the Rue Morgue" to discuss Poe's horror stories, I will now detour from my account of his horror stories to talk about horror in general—for my model in this chapter is not a theorem in mathematics or the 100-yard dash, but Freud's *Moses and Monotheism,* in which a thread is un-ravelled, then dropped, another picked up, unravelled, then dropped, a third picked up, unravelled, and then tied to the others into a neat knot, right around our necks. This digression is in the mood of Halloween, a time when the sleep of reason leads to every sort of divagation from the straight and narrow.

"Halloween is the carnival-time of disembodied spirits," said Nathaniel Hawthorne, who knew what he was talking about. A proper carnival is a rite of disinhibition, a riot of release, a good time for letting go, for letting out what you normally keep in. That is what makes Halloween fun. What makes Halloween scary is the nature of the spirits that are let out. They are re-embodiments of our secret fears and desires, of monstrous hungers and frightful lusts. Ghosts, ghouls, witches, incubi, succubi, vampires, werewolves, possessive demons and demonic children are figures combining fascination, repulsion, and threat. They are fascinating because they are representatives of a suppressed wish; repulsive because we consider the wish shameful or disgusting; and threatening because we expect to be punished for the wish. Halloween threatens with what it promises, like a vampire puckering up for a kiss.

The literary equivalent of Halloween is horror fiction, in which re-embodied spirits solicit and scare us with a sinister and insinuating allure. In honor of Halloween, I should like to celebrate these spirits, not by abandoning myself to them, but—and this is how it goes with those of us who live by (or through) the word—by talking about them.

Among the many oddities of our emotional life, the *frisson* of horror is one of the oddest. In the first place, it is usually a response to something that is not there. Under normal circumstances, that is, it attends only such things as nightmares, hallucinations, phobias, and literature. In that respect it is unlike *terror*, for instance, which is extreme and sudden fear in the face of a material threat. If coming around a corner on a path in Central Park, you find yourself face to face with a lion snarling and crouched for a spring, you feel terror. The terror can be dissipated by a SWAT team with flamethrowers or by a scramble up a tree. *Horror*, on the other hand, is extreme and sudden fear in the face of an immaterial cause. The frights of nightmares, daymares, and nightmarish literature cannot be dissipated by a SWAT team; to flee them is to run into them at every new turn.

Phobias, sure enough, seem to have material causes. But if you have a phobia of earmuffs or peaches, say, of toad stools or dripping faucets, it is because they are convenient retainers for some meaning you have invested in them. It is what they remind you of that horrifies you, not what they are materially. A person in the grip of a phobia is hallucinating a memory he has forced himself to forget.

There are indeed times when a sinister conspiracy of coincidences seems to echo or expose our thoughts, or worse, seems produced by them—when, that is, the effect of horror is caused by something actually there. We all have our bouts of paranoia, when our most abysmal fears and fantasies seem to become flesh. I gather from the accounts of those who have recovered, or from the recorded speech of those who have not, that paranoid schizophrenia is a condition of sustained horror; the whole world becomes your phobia, as though you were a character in a story by Poe or Kafka, as though you were Leopold Bloom in the Circe episode of *Ulysses*. Madness, in spite of those who champion it as the higher sanity, is always horrifying, in literature and in life. It is a horror to the sane because it is a temptation to let it all hang out; it is a horror to the insane because it feels like a punishment for letting it all hang out. Before the twentieth century, at least, we hid madmen away, I suggest, largely because of what they revealed to us about ourselves.

We have come far enough for an attempt at a preliminary definition. Horror resides in an image, or object, or situation that evokes for a perceiver the substance of his nightmares, or repressed wishes made fearful by repression. Different people, of course, are bedeviled by different nightmares. Some people claim not to have nightmares at all (but my guess is that they are kidding either us or themselves). It follows that different objects and situations are nightmarish to different people. *The Exorcist* got to Mary, but not to John, who had palpitations while watching *Psycho*. And some people, the aliens among us no doubt, seem entirely immune to the infectious chills of all horror fiction. Just the same, I believe that of the popular genres horror fiction cuts widest along the lines of class, occupation, sex, and educational level. Fans of westerns may be turned off by romances, and readers of harlequins may wonder what anyone sees in science fiction, but the traits that keep these groups of readers apart will not seal off a susceptibility to horror, which is not affected by social barriers.

In any case, we immediately recognize scenes that are supposed to provoke horror, no matter how we feel about them. A child watching his first horror movie does not have to be told when to hide under his seat. The conventions of horror fiction and films, I conclude, are metaphors for very common fantasies of mixed fear and desire that we already know from the inside. These conventions are few in number, although infinitely variable.

Here are a few actual or synthetic instances: (1) A timid and lovelorn ventriloquist gradually succumbs to the will of his raunchy, wisecracking, and immortal dummy. (2) The benevolent, philanthropic, and very proper Dr. Jekyll decides to try a new potion on himself. (3) Mr. Griffen, who gives up medicine to study physics, learns how to make himself invisible; the drugs involved, however, bring out what is worst in his character. (4) There is a pair of twins, both beautiful, one good, one evil; but who knows which is which? Even they are not sure. (5) Under a harvest moon, shy and mild-mannered Larry Talbot hates what is happening to him, but cannot prevent his canines and a pelt from sprouting; he howls at the moon.

These are all metaphors of dissociation: what is sane, tame, and daylit in us gives in, loses control, to what in us we consider evil and monstrous, to appetites we have good reason for keeping out of sight and out of mind. The wages of this sin are madness and death.

Or take another convention with its variants: (1) A pubescent girl is inhabited by Satan; she curses, blasphemes, and stabs herself in the privates with a crucifix. (2) Carrie, after her first menses, develops magical powers; she uses them to destroy her enemies and the town they live in. (3) A nubile woman is taken over by (a) a computer, (b) a demonic or dead lover, (c) the fetus she is carrying, begot in a nightmare by Satan, and (d) a spirit long resident in a picturesque old house the woman just moved into. She thereupon begins to misbehave. (4) Aliens from outer space scoop out the minds and souls of human beings; they occupy the space left vacant. You can always spot an alien, for it lacks the ordinary human emotions. All it wants is power, control—it is an unfeeling and immoral appetite we cannot master. All the reason, morality, and fine feelings we are so proud of cannot deter its implacable progress. These instances suggest something we already know from other sources: whatever possesses you comes from within; it seems to come from without because we can't or won't acknowledge it. A person trying to fight off an attack of dissociation must feel as though he were possessed.

In real life, hunchbacks, dwarfs, midgets, fat ladies, and the skeletal man are just folks like the rest of us. In horror fiction and in the recesses of our minds they are reminders of our freakish inner lives. Similarly, homosexuals, hermaphrodites, and transvestites bear the burden of desires we fear in ourselves. All sexual perversions are horrifying to those who do not have them, and perhaps to those who do, if we are to judge from recent homosexual novels. Since all human sex is tinged with perversion, all human sex can be depicted as horrifying. He: "Do you think sex is dirty?" She: "When it's done right." The Reverend Davidson was horrified by what he did with Sadie Tomkins, although it was nothing out of the ordinary.

Haunted houses are phobias writ large. They reflect the condition of childhood, when whatever house we lived in was haunted. The two most famous haunted houses of fiction, Rochester's fire trap in *Jane Eyre* and the equally combustible chateau in *Rebecca,* are the scenes of fantasies in which girls supplant their mad, bad, and sexy mothers in the affections of their fathers.

Horror story plots revolving around the demonic potential of children would be: (1) A pretty little girl lives in a neat little house with her beautiful mommy and her handsome daddy. She's a cute little devil. It is a shame that someone killed her snoopy little brother and her rival at school. (2) In the sewer system of a great city, in an abandoned tenement, or in a cave in Central Park, a pack of children munch on the bones of their latest victim. (3) During a night of inexplicable electrical disturbances all the women of childbearing age become pregnant; nine months later they deliver whiz kids who show no affection, no feeling of any kind, for their parents or anyone else. They aspire to nothing but complete control over everything on earth. (4) Little Damien has a ferocious black dog as playmate and protector: with his tricycle he knocks his mother over a balustrade; hidden under his neat black hair is a birthmark shaped like the number 666.

Children become demonic during those moments when we can't help seeing that they are less innocent than we officially pretend. One critic observed that horror fiction is strictly for the kids—but only because he could imagine nothing more dreadful than the fantasy life of an adolescent boy. More often, children become demonic when we attribute to them the evil wishes, of various kinds, that they inspire in us. It is no longer news that children are frequently molested, nor that even the best of parents secretly feel that their little vampires are draining them dry. Tales of demonic children are written mostly by women; tales of demonic women are written mostly by men.

Other horror fiction concentrates on the theme of the living dead: (1) On London's lamplit streets King Tut's mummy walks. That girl he is carrying, the one in the diaphanous dress, has fainted. (2) On a Carribbean island zombies stalk the living. (3) A tomb stone tilts; the earth crumbles open; a bony arm reaches out to grab you. (4) Atomic testing rouses the dead, who have a taste for human flesh, particularly the liver.

We fear the living dead as we fear corpses and skeletons, because we fear death. We fear death for a number of reasons, some reasonable, such as that we like life, some irrational, such as the superstition that death is a punishment for sin. We fear the dead simply because we are living, because we assume that the dead have a grudge against us. We have all wished someone dead, or at least thought "better you than me." We fear the living dead because they are like aliens—apparitions of appetite without feelings or conscience or restraint. The living dead are mixed figures of our ghastly longings and the punishment for them. We fear dissociation because it involves the death of the ego. But then for a religious person death is only a variety of dissociations.

The dolls, mannikins, wax works, and dummies of horror fiction are like the living dead, in that they are normally insentient things that have become animate, all the better to act out their designs upon us, which are our own. They are like masks and magic mirrors, in that they reveal to us what we otherwise don't see, the *risus sardonicus* we can't turn our faces around to face. The melting faces of *Westworld* and *Alien* are related—mobile human features dissolving to reveal the rigid and malevolent automaton within. These dolls, mirrors, and melting faces are like the attendant animals in horror fiction in that they are estranged and uncanny versions of familiar things. A wolf is an uncanny dog, man's best friend become nocturnal and predatory. Bats are eerie parodies of birds, as are owls, both predatory creatures of the night. Rats and mice are wild animals that act as though they belong in our houses, in which at night they romp like bad dreams.

Like Freud's uncanny, these animals are all both familiar and alien, domestic and wild, *heimlich* and *unheimlich*. And like all the other literary horrors I have surveyed, they are representations of either dissociation or projection, or both at once, when they appear in fiction or in the life of our imagination, as distinct from the life outside our imaginations, assuming there is any.

Fine. But all that still does not explain what horror is good for, or why certain classes of images and situations stimulate it. Since as well as being a half-baked Freudian, I am a half-baked Darwinian, I shall give an evolutionary answer. Once again, a comparison with terror will help us out. Terror I would guess is the emotional concomitant to the body's getting ready for flight in the face of a sudden and unconquerable threat. It is what we feel when those secretions flow, the bowels loosen, and muscles tense. It helped us to survive in a natural environment that at one time was more dangerous than we are—it evolved, that is, in response to extraspecific selective pressures. But some of every animal's physical traits, behavior patterns, and emotions evolved in response to conspecific selective pressures, to pressures exerted on an animal by the other members of its species. Take, for example, the tails of peacocks and the equally gorgeous behinds of baboons. Neither attraction is of much use to peacocks and baboons in their struggle with nature; their function, rather, is to stimulate meaningful interpersonal relations. Whether female peacocks and baboons experience the emotion of love when they spot these come-ons we don't know, but they act as though they do. In any case, when human males are stimulated by the homologous portions of their female conspecifics they feel an emotion we might as well call love, while their bodies get ready for it. Similarly, *horror* evolved intraspecifically as the emotional concomitant to the breaking of a taboo. The feeling of horror is a signal that we are indulging actually or imaginatively in something we have forbidden ourselves, usually for the sake of the group. The bodily weakness, numbness, feeling of suffocation, and inability to move prevents us from indulging ourselves further. A phobia, by the way, is close to being a personalized taboo.

Having thus in seven sentences established my lack of credentials as a scientist, I shall detour back to literature, to Poe's horror stories. We are now in a position to see that "William Wilson" is in one crucial respect the opposite of all the other stories alluded to in my catalogue of horrors. In tales of ventriloquists, Jekylls and Hydes, Dorian Grays, werewolves, demonic possession, aliens, the walking dead, and creeping whatnot, the portion of the self that is split off or projected is evil, appetitive, monstrous, somehow *lower*. In Poe's story, the self that is split off, the second William Wilson, is ethical, self-effacing, a counsel of restraint, intelligent, somehow *higher*. It is the conscious ego, the portion of the self that thinks of itself as the entire self, that is evil and criminal. But it is the conscience that is horrifying. Poe's positioning of us, however, his giving over of the narrative to the criminal ego, forces us to sympathize, perhaps even to identify with it—and with its evil projects. Such is the moral topography of all of Poe's best horror stories.

Consider "The Imp of the Perverse," which also begins as though it were an essay. An agitated speaker seems to be delivering a treatise on some previously unknown propensity of the human soul. "In the pure arrogance of the reason," he says, "we have all overlooked it." We have overlooked it "simply because of its supererogation," because it is gratuitous, absurd, because we could see no need for it. Yet the speaker is sure that this impulse or propensity is "radical, primitive, irreducible," a *primum mobile* that is not *motivirt,* a motive without a motive, a first cause without a cause, a refutation in itself of the argument from design. For want of a better term, our speaker calls this irresistible drive perverseness, the Imp of the Perverse. "I am not more certain that I breathe," he says "than that the assurance of the wrong or error of any action is often the one unconquerable *force* which impels us, and alone impels us to its prosecution. Nor will this overwhelming tendency to do wrong for the wrong's sake, admit of analysis, of resolution into ulterior elements."

Among a number of illustrations, this is the most striking:

We stand upon the brink of a precipice. We peer into the abyss—we grow sick and dizzy. Our first impulse is to shrink from the danger. Unaccountably we remain. By slow degrees our sickness, and dizziness, and horror, become merged in a cloud of unnameable feeling. By gradations, still more imperceptible, this cloud assumes shape, as did the vapor from the bottle out of which arose the genius of the Arabian Nights. But out of this *our* cloud upon the precipice's edge, there grows into palpability, a shape, far more terrible than any genius, or any demon of a tale, and yet it is but a thought, although a fearful one, and one which chills the very marrow of our bones with the fierceness of the delight of its horror. It is merely the idea of what would be our sensations during the sweeping precipitancy of a fall from such a height. And this fall—this rushing annihilation—for the very reason that it involves that one most ghastly and loathsome of all the most ghastly and loathsome images of death and suffering which have ever presented themselves to our imagination—for this very cause we now most vividly desire it. And because our reason violently deters us from the brink, *therefore,* do we the most impetuously approach it. There is no passion in nature so demonically impatient, as that of him, who shuddering upon the edge of precipice, thus meditates a plunge. To indulge for a moment, in any attempt at *thought,* is to be inevitably lost; for reflection but urges us to forbear, and *therefore* it is, I say, that we *cannot.* If there be no friendly arm to check us, or if we fail in a sudden effort to prostrate ourselves backward from the abyss, we plunge, and are destroyed.

Abruptly, the dissertation breaks off, and we are plunged into a narrative. The speaker confesses to us that he has committed a crime, a

perfect crime, in fact, a murder. His means was a poisoned candle; for
years now he has been living high in perfect security on the fortune he
inherited from his victim. It is impossible that anyone should ever find
him out. It is just that of late he has been harassed and haunted by a
phrase that he can't stop repeating under his breath, the phrase "I am
safe." Here is how the story ends:

One day, while sauntering along the streets, I arrested myself in the act of
murmuring, half aloud, these customary syllables. In a fit of petulance, I re-
modelled them thus:—'I am safe—I am safe—yes—if I be not fool enough to
make open confession!'

No sooner had I spoken these words, than I felt an icy chill creep to my heart.
I had had some experience in these fits of perversity, (whose nature I have been
at some trouble to explain,) and I remembered well, that in no instance, I had
successfully resisted their attacks. And now my own casual self-suggestion, that
I might possibly be fool enough to confess the murder of which I had been
guilty, confronted me, as if the very ghost of him whom I had murdered—and
beckoned me on to death.

At first, I made an effort to shake off this nightmare of the soul. I walked
vigorously—faster—still faster—at length I ran. I felt a maddening desire to
shriek aloud. Every succeeding wave of thought overwhelmed me with new
terror, for alas! I well, too well, understood that to *think* in my situation, was to
be lost. I still quickened my pace. I bounded like a madman through the
crowded thoroughfares. At length, the populace took the alarm, and pursued
me. I felt then the consummation of my fate. Could I have torn out my tongue, I
would have done it—but a rough voice resounded in my ears—a rougher grasp
seized me by the shoulder. I turned—I gasped for breath. For a moment, I
experienced all the pangs of suffocation; I became blind, and deaf, and giddy;
and then, some invisible fiend, I thought, struck me with his broad palm upon
the back. The long-imprisoned secret burst forth from my soul.

They say that I spoke with a distinct enunciation, but with marked emphasis
and passionate hurry, as if in dread of interruption before concluding the brief
but pregnant sentences that consigned me to the hangman and to hell.

Having related all that was necessary for the fullest judicial conviction, I fell
prostrate in a swoon.

But why shall I say more? To-day I wear these chains, and am *here*. To-
morrow I shall be fetterless!—*but where?*

Poe's Imp of the Perverse is once again equivalent to the conscience,
although this time it becomes manifest not in a double, but in a
compulsion to confess. Just the same, its victim experiences it first as a
possessing demon or imp and then as a projected "invisible hand," a

dissociated ghost of his repressed guilt that grabs him by the shoulder, whispers in his ear, and slaps him on the back, thus making him cough up his secret. Once again the conscious persona is criminal, and the conscience is alien and horrifying. Similar stories are "The Black Cat," in which the narrator's conscience is projected onto first one black cat, and then onto another, and "The Tell-Tale Heart," in which the narrator's guilt is projected onto an old man's "eye of a vulture—a pale blue eye, with a film over it." In both stories the narrator literally gets away with murder until the Imp of the Perverse forces him to reveal to the police his victim's corpse. But the most celebrated and most complex of Poe's tales of dissociation is "The Fall of the House of Usher," in which all the characters are aspects of each other.

As usual, the narrator is anonymous, but the most self-aware portion of that single mind within which the story occurs goes by the name Roderick Usher. Critics have long observed that Roderick Usher looks exactly like Edgar Allan Poe. Here is how the narrator describes him:

A cadaverousness of complexion; an eye large, liquid, and luminous beyond comparison; lips somewhat thin and very pallid, but of a surpassingly beautiful curve; a nose of delicate Hebrew model, but with a breadth of nostril unusual in similar formations; a finely moulded chin, speaking, in its want of prominence, of a want of moral energy; hair of a more than web-like softness and tenuity; these features, with an inordinate expansion above the regions of the temple, made up altogether a countenance not easily to be forgotten.

Usher has summoned the narrator to sit with him through a bout with an indefinable "mental disorder." He is nearly out of his mind with depression and dread, with unassigned horror. Nothing in particular aroused Usher's dread, but everything increases it, as unconsciously he arranges his own dissolution. Usher fears no particular danger; he fears only fear itself. "The period will sooner or later arrive," he tells the narrator, "when I must abandon life and reason together, in some struggle with the grim phantasm, FEAR." Usher's fear is contagious; his mind, says the narrator, is one "from which darkness, as of an inherent positive quality, poured forth upon all objects of the moral and physical universe in one unceasing radiation of gloom."

Usher's horror of horror infects the narrator, who begins to share Usher's hallucinations. It infects Usher's twin sister, who falls into catalepsy and is buried alive by Usher. It infects all of the "House of

Usher," the name given by local people to both the family and the building they have lived in for generations. The house, looking with its "vacant and eye-like windows" like a human face from the outside, is reflected in a lurid and lustrous tarn that lies beside it, and resembles Usher in that a crack runs through it from top to bottom. Aware of the connection, Usher has constructed a theory of the sentience of all matter, especially the house. At the end, Usher dies of horror as his sister in her final death agonies falls upon him and bears them both to the floor as corpses. The house then splits along its crack and crumbles into the tarn.

I think it is fair to say that what Usher fears and dies of is dissociation—although his death may be taken as a metaphor for the conscious self's submergence into another self that then comes to the surface. And what makes Usher so polymorphously susceptible to dissociation is his artistic genius. We get a close look at one of his paintings—of the interior of a funeral vault, like the one in which he inters his sister. We hear of his prodigious musical virtuosity, especially of his long improvised dirges. We read one of his poems, "The Haunted Palace," in which the palace figures as an extended simile for a mind that moves from a sane and harmonious happiness to a discordant and desolate madness. To Poe, an artist was above all someone with an imagination. And for him an artistic imagination was not just a capacity for forming images, but a capacity for projection. Poe's artists, like Keat's Shakespeare, has "negative capability"; he distributes himself among the subject of his art. He breaks off so much of himself into all he renders, into all he imagines, that a point comes at which he cannot pull himself together again. Poe's version of the old notion of a connection between madness and genius thus has a certain specificity. To have genius is to have an imagination. To have an imagination is to have a personality without boundaries, to see yourself or put yourself into whatever your imagination seizes on. To have an imagination is to dissociate. To dissociate is to go mad. There is no way of getting out of your mind; there is no way of resisting its processes. In the artist's attempt to get out of his mind, he goes out of it—he falls apart.

We are now ready for our last detour, back to our point of origin, "The Murders in the Rue Morgue," to the horror that Dupin subdues by analysis. He and his companion first learn of this horror through newspaper reports of the murder of Madame L'Espanaye and her daughter in a fourth-floor apartment on the Rue Morgue:

The apartment was in the wildest disorder—the furniture broken and thrown about in all directions. There was only one bedstead; and from this the bed had been removed, and thrown into the middle of the floor. On a chair lay a razor, besmeared with blood. On the hearth were two or three long and thick tresses of grey human hair, also dabbled in blood, and seeming to have been pulled out by the roots. Upon the floor were found four Napoleons, an ear-ring of topaz, three large silver spoons, three smaller of *metal d'Alger,* and two bags, containing nearly four thousand francs in gold. The drawers of a bureau, which stood in one corner, were open, and had been, apparently, rifled, although many articles still remained in them. A small iron safe was discovered under the bed (not under the bedstead). It was open with the key still in the door. It had no contents beyond a few old letters, and other paper of little consequence.

Of Madame L'Espanaye no traces were here seen; but an unusual quantity of soot being observed in the fire-place, a search was made in the chimney, and (horrible to relate!) the corpse of the daughter, head downward, was dragged therefrom; it having been thus forced up the narrow aperture for a considerable distance. The body was quite warm. Upon examining it, many excoriations were perceived, no doubt occasioned by the violence with which it had been thrust up and disengaged. Upon the face were many severe scratches, and, upon the throat, dark bruises, and deep indentations of finger nails, as if the deceased had been throttled to death.

After a thorough investigation of every portion of the house, without farther discovery, the party made its way into a small paved yard in the rear of the building, where lay the corpse of the old lady, with her throat so entirely cut that, upon an attempt to raise her, the head fell off. The body, as well as the head, was fearfully mutilated—the former so much so as scarcely to retain any semblance of humanity.

To this horrible mystery there is not as yet, we believe, the slightest clew.

The police are baffled: so far as they can tell there was no way for the murderer either to get in or get out, for the doors and windows were all locked from the inside. Was some demon at work? But Dupin is resolutely secular—"It is not too much to say that neither of us believe in præternatural events," he observes to his companion. He determines the means of ingress and egress by observation and logic. But he determines the identity of the murderer by the analytic method, which, as you recall, involves identifying himself with the mind he is trying to master. After a long exposition, he sums things up for the narrator:

we have gone so far as to combine the ideas of an agility astounding, a strength superhuman, a ferocity brutal, a butchery without motive, a *grotesquerie* in horror absolutely alien from humanity, and a voice foreign in tone to the ears of men of many nations. . . . What impression have I made upon your fancy?

The narrator feels his flesh creep. "A madman," he says, "has done this deed—some raving maniac, escaped from a neighboring *Maison de Santé*." "In some respects," responds Dupin, "your idea is not irrelevant." He shows the narrator some long red hairs found at the scene of the crime and then points out to him a passage from Cuvier:

It was a minute anatomical and generally descriptive account of the large fulvous Ourang-Outang of the East Indian Islands. The gigantic stature, the prodigious strength and activity, the wild ferocity, and the imitative propensities of these mammalia are sufficiently well known to all.

Reading this passage, says the narrator, "I understood the full horrors of the murder at once."

But I am not sure that our unimaginative narrator understands half of it. The wild ferocity and imitative propensities of orangutans may have been well known to all, but not from observation. Poe is far from the only nineteenth-century writer to use one of the great apes as a stand-in for what is still primitive, ferocious, and insane in the most exalted of creatures, the one made in God's image. Poe's orangutan is one with horrors I discussed earlier, another product of dissociation and projection. Dupin, the highest of men, recognizes himself in the subhuman orangutan; the police do not; they are above all unimaginative—which in this case means out of touch with themselves.

We later learn from the beast's owner, a sailor, what happened on the night of the murders. Coming home one night from a carouse, he found the beast broken out of his closet, razor in hand, fully lathered, trying to shave, in imitation of its master. The sailor reaches for his whip; the ape flees; the sailor pursues; the ape clambers up a lightening rod and into the room of the two women; the sailor follows it up the rod, looks in the window, and "nearly fell from his hold through excess of horror," Here's what he sees:

the gigantic animal had seized Madame L'Espanaye by the hair, (which was loose, as she had been combing it,) and was flourishing the razor about her face, in imitation of the motions of a barber. The daughter lay prostrate and motionless; she had swooned. The screams and struggles of the old lady (during which the hair was torn from her head) had the effect of changing the probably pacific purposes of the Ourang-Outang into those of wrath. With one determined sweep of its muscular arm it nearly severed her head from her body. The sight of blood inflamed its anger into phrenzy. Gnashing its teeth, and flashing fire from its eyes, it flew upon the body of the girl, and imbedded its fearful talons in her throat, retaining its grasp until she expired. Its wandering and wild glances fell at this moment upon the head of the bed, over which the face of its master, rigid with horror, was just discernible. The fury of the beast, who no doubt bore still in mind the dreaded whip, was instantly converted into fear. Conscious of having deserved punishment, it seemed desirous of concealing its bloody deeds, and skipped about the chamber in an agony of nervous agitation; throwing down and breaking the furniture as it moved, and dragging the bed from the bedstead. In conclusion, its seized first the corpse of the daughter, and thrust it up the chimney, as it was found; then that of the old lady, which it immediately hurled through the window headlong.

The ape in this passage is not ferocious by nature, but by nurture, or rather by the lack of it. His original intentions, we read, were "probably pacific." He is made ferocious by confinement and the whip, by fear and guilt, by horror in the gaze of the humans he emulates. But at the outset, the orangutan wanted no more than to ape its master, to become human. In all these respects Poe's orangutan is different from the figures in my earlier catalog of horrors, all of which were implacable in their malevolence from the outset. Although the ape is a representation of something abysmal and inhuman in humanity, some system of primitive appetites split off and projected onto a figure of horror, Poe seems to recognize that it was made into a horror by oppression. Poe does not, as would most writers of horror fiction, destroy his monster, but finds a home for it in a botanical garden. There's a moral here, but I refuse to draw it.

Instead, I should like to point to a kind of logic in the fact that the world's greatest writer of horror fiction also invented the detective story. Poe's horror stories, although fantastic in method, are informed by the reality principle: this is how it goes with us. His detective stories, although realistic in method, are informed by the pleasure principle: this is how I wish things went with us. Dupin is imaginative; he dissociates at will; he is sympathetically attuned to the horrors he exorcises and the criminals he exposes. Without Dupin, the horrors within would destroy us. Without Dupin, since God no longer enters the picture, the wicked would go free and the good would be punished. In "The Murders in the Rue Morgue," the police arrest a man named Adolphe Le Bon for the murders of the two women. This innocent's name not only sounds like "Auguste Dupin"; it also means "Adolph the good." Dupin is our savior; in his sight, we wear windows in our bosoms, as we did in the sight of the original Savior, recently absconded. It is precisely because Poe knew how much we need to be saved, how little we are able to save ourselves, that he invented detective stories in which the horrors that otherwise destroy us are analyzed out of existence. For similar reasons, no doubt, Freud invented himself.

But my charge in this chapter, as I understand it, is not to reach conclusions, but to provoke discussion. I shall therefore conclude not with an assertion, but with a question: Why is the idea of drowning in water terrifying, while the idea of sinking into quicksand is horrifying?

Notes

1. Stuart and Susan Levine, eds., *The Short Fiction of Edgar Allan Poe.* (Indianapolis: Bobbs-Merrill, 1976), p. 153.
2. The definition is by Thomas Ollive Mabbott, ed., in *The Collected Works of Edgar Allan Poe, Tales and Sketches, 1831–1842.* (Cambridge: Harvard University Press, 1978), p. 185. All E. A. Poe quotations in the text come from this edition.

8. Comments on Post-Traumatic Stress Disorder and Dissociation

Lawrence C. Kolb, M.D.

In this chapter, I would like to discuss recent research on the ways in which horrifying experiences precipitate self-disorganization. During World War II, I worked extensively with acute cases of war neurosis. The variation in the clinical material was tremendous, ranging from those individuals who were seriously impaired and dissociated to those with a subsiding expression of terror sometimes called anxiety. The current experience with Vietnam veterans is very different and most interesting, in the sense that one observes in the chronic states of Post-Traumatic Stress Disorder (PTSD) the complicated effects of reflection upon original experiences and the continuing suffering from fear-induced somatic symptoms. The chronic states are quite different from the consequences of an immediate, terrible, terror-stricken event in which the individual suddenly perceives the truth of his vulnerability: he is about to die or be seriously maimed. At the same moment, he discovers the truth about himself. However he has pictured his role as a warrior, it is destroyed. He now knows he is not the heroic warrior. He may picture himself suddenly as a coward, or as a weakling, or as whatever he might have secretly thought about himself. It is at this moment that his self-concept can be destroyed. Now he must live with the new realization and the consequences of his experience are considerable.

Many face another more immediate problem: somatic consequences of the experience. I was surprised to find that Vietnam veterans 10 or 15 years after the war had a "startle" reaction to a particular noise.[1] The startle reflex is indigenous to every infant and probably to every living form. It has been closely studied in years past; it may be conditioned to associated sounds, sights, or odors. It was remarkable 10, 15, or 20 years after the combat event to hear men tell about suddenly hearing a loud noise reminding them of battle sounds and then being in a panic state. Some men even said that following such noises they felt suddenly they weren't themselves.

With this in mind and commencing treatment, we exposed some men to a modified narcosynthetic procedure. Rather than verbally suggesting an image of being on the battlefield we simply played a tape of meaningful noise consisting of combat sounds, including those of helicopters, mortars, and screaming wounded. Thinking there would be some somatic accompaniments, we made an attempt to record those responses with a polygraph and EEG. There was no question we could immediately produce a dissociation. The patients immediately returned to a critical event in the battlefield. Many then experienced and reenacted scenes of fight, flight, or rage. Unfortunately, taking the drug obliterated any physiological responsivity. So convinced was I this must occur that, in collaboration with Professor Blanchard of the State University of New York, we then exposed fully conscious Vietnam veterans as well as a number of control groups to a train of combat sounds lasting thirty seconds.[2] The subjects could turn off the stimulus if they wanted to and we could vary it in intensity over a period of time. To date, about 60 individuals have been exposed to this test. As controls we also exposed Vietnam-era veterans who were never in Vietnam, Vietnam noncombatant veterans, Vietnam veterans with other psychiatric disorders, civilians with anxiety states, and same age non-Vietnam young people. The Vietnam combat veterans with PTSD responded to the intellectual stress tests just like the controls. When it came to the combat sound exposure though, it was quite evident that this group responded in a significant way, with immediate rises in both systolic and diastolic blood pressure and pulse rate as well as in muscle tension.

It is interesting that about 10 percent of our patients come from our pain clinic. Clinicians could not understand why they complained extensively about their pain. One might suggest that excessive muscular tension had something to do with it. Under the narcosynthetic process, these people revealed other things they had repressed: they have a propensity to dissociate when given mind-altering drugs. In taking histories you also learn that some combat veterans with PTSD, when operated upon, dissociate during the recovery period. They would be told afterward by the anesthetist that they were "crazy." According to the anesthetists, the patients yelled, screamed, and fought while pulling off the life support systems. Many of the men in this study described incidents on social occasions in which they might take a drink or some mind-altering drug and someone would come up behind and touch them. In the next moment, they would become dissociated and sometimes engage in a fight. Often these incidents were reported in newspapers the next day, with statements that they had grabbed a gun or knife and seemingly threatened someone. In fact, they were defending themselves from an imaginary but nonexistent enemy.

Other researchers have also conducted research. Malloy, Fairbank, and Keane in Mississippi have studied ten cases but used a different stimulus.[3] They applied both visual and auditory stimuli related to combat scenes and discovered similar immediate psychophysiologic responses as in our laboratory. In another study from World War II, Dodds and Wilson compared 20 patients with 20 college students.[4] They separated their combat veterans with chronic combat fatigue into those who were socially adapted and those who were socially maladapted. The maladapted group were not even able to finish watching the combat movies used as a stimulus. Many fled the laboratory. In our experiment, many of our subjects stopped the experiment at a certain level of sound intensity, wept, or said they could not go on. My interpretation is that these men have a conditioned emotional response to a meaningful life-threatening stimulus. The primitive startle reflex has been conditioned to associated stimuli experienced repeatedly on the battlefield.

How may we comprehend these clinical and laboratory observations? Freud was terribly upset when his colleagues described to him the clinical symptomatology of the war neurosis. He recognized that both his libido theory and his dream theory were threatened. He declared this neurosis was a simple traumatic neurosis.[5]

My observations suggest that war neuroses are among the most complex neuroses that exist. One gets involved not only in fixation to a primitive, childlike learning process through conditioning to startle but also in the complexities of an adult personality attempting to control excessive somatic arousal on exposure to hitherto meaningless external stimuli as well as to internally traumatic imaging.[1]

As a product of his thinking about war neuroses, Freud conceived and described the stimulus barrier.[6] As he did so, he pointed out that man has evolved from his peripheral protective barrier (he described both the skin and the contact sensory barrier as such) and erected a central barrier within the central nervous system to protect him from excessive excitation.

We know very little of the effects of highly intensive stimulation—emotional stimulation—upon the cortical neuronal structure, that is, the central barrier. I think we might conceive of the fact that we could learn something from examining the effects of such stimulation upon the contact sensory barrier. There is a fine literature on the effects of excessive stimulation on the auditory system.[7] The people in otolaryngology talk about threshold impairments, episodic impairments, and permanent impairments following exposure to high intensity noise of varying duration. They have shown by very detailed experimentation that one may develop temporary changes in structure, ongoing changes in structure, and permanent changes in structure (both anatomical and neurochemical structure) in the internal ear following such exposures. My speculation is that the stimulus barrier now buried in the cerebral cortex (and I suspect it is in the limbic system) may undergo the same kind of changes in the face of excessive excitation. Some experiments on cortical function due to excessive emotional arousal in others more severely exposed to the process of horror-terror over long periods of time show that permanent defects probably occur of the kind observable in the external sensory system.

We now classify the chronic patients we see as mild, moderate, or severe. I have not seen any patient recover from the evidence of pathologic processing of their terror-induced images, that is, the recurrent dreams or the intrusive thinking. Is it possible to provide an explanatory statement about that? I think so. There are portions of the hind brains concerned with dreaming, sleep, and agnostic activity. These contain the highest levels of neuroadrenergic substances—the locus coeruleus and related structures. I postulate that this section of the brain might be released in the face of a temporary or permanent impairment of cortical inhibitory control and therefore continually make available excitation to produce agnostic dreaming, or thinking, imaging material. Thinking along these lines we have prescribed for our patients adrenergic blocking agents which cause some attenuation of these symptoms.[8] Personally, I do not think we can realize complete control of such symptoms since we have both a deficit as well as a release problem.

I happen to suffer from an auditory problem in my left ear well known to otologists. Anyone who uses a shotgun is eventually going to suffer a hightone deafness if they do not protect the ear. If they use a rifle the deafness will occur in the right ear. I never used the protective devices. I know some individuals who have used shotguns for many years and they are absolutely stone deaf, yet I am not. I have certain deficit symptoms but I have release symptoms as well. I have to struggle with the deficit symptoms as I have to use a hearing prosthesis in order to hear. I also suffer a release symptom; the constant buzzing in my ear, the tinnitus. My guess is that individuals with PTSD who are suffering the consequences of overwhelming terror-induced stimulation also suffer both deficit and release symptoms, but then they also have the other puzzling personality problems.

Why are such patients often diagnosed as schizophrenic? Why are they called manic depressive? Why are they called anxiety states? I think each sufferer calls into play here all the psychological defensive measures embodied in his personality structure in his attempt to bring about inhibition and control of aggressivity. No wonder the clinical picture is so complex.

In chapter 5, by Frank Putnam, I was fascinated by the analysis of the phenomenon of multiple personalities from a structural physiological point of view. The people he sees give a history of dreadful experiences in early childhood. The people I see are adults, young adults, who have had dreadful experiences at a particular moment in their early adulthood. Their personality structure is pretty well constructed, for the most part, although we see a few who come to us with developmental histories suggesting sizable immaturity at the time of exposure to intense trauma.

How does it happen that some adults develop PTSD and others do not? Young people and older people are considered more prone to develop PTSD. Probably the cortical inhibitory barrier is less developed or activated in these age groups. From the literature about followup of the chronic cases from World War II, one would suspect that persons who have psychologically traumatic experiences in early life suffer a change in their capacity to inhibit intensive emotions.[9] Thus they are predisposed to further damage when re-exposed.

To proceed to another matter: One of the questions raised is, why are we seeing so many people today with dissociative states? From the chapter by Dr. Hannah Decker, we can wonder how it happened that physicians became interested in these phenomena around 1882. I inquired of Dr. Decker about possible war experiences in France prior to this time which might have increased the likelihood of many more people in the population being prone to depersonalization at the same time. I was interested in a period of tremendous terror and horror for individuals and asked her about the Franco-Prussian War. She immediately identified the date and described the Prussian artillery siege of Paris which continued for months. Is it possible that in Paris, ten years or so after the Franco-Prussian War, there were large numbers of people predisposed by their intense overstimulation to dissociate through changes in their neuronal structure? We are looking now at a group of young people in this country who are ten to fifteen years beyond the terror of Vietnam.

I think it would be very interesting to examine mercenaries. We have looked at some men who re-enlisted after an original tour of combat duty and returned to Vietnam for more. Some had survival guilt and returned in an attempt to get killed. Others went back for excitation so that they might once again re-exercise the great sense of power they had felt. Their psychological break in the second tour came after the death or killing of a buddy. Suddenly they recognized their vulnerability. Some became catatonoid at that time. As I see them clinically today, those people exposed for long periods of time are now the most severely disturbed. We did not learn very much from a psychiatric point of view from World War II. In Vietnam many men were sent back to the line after collapse and treatment at frontline aid stations. The military medical fraternity made many statements that the high rate of return to combat through frontline psychiatric intervention was a great success. It may have been seen as a great success to get a man back on the line. These people, however, were exposed once again to tremendously threatening stimulation. At a certain point many broke. We now see many with chronic or delayed casualities of the war. My impression is that the number of chronic cases from Vietnam is greater than from either the Korean or World War II conflicts.

Notes

Dr. Kolb's remarks were based upon past studies and a current one, "From Process to Pathology: Chronic Post-Traumatic Stress Disorder of Central Inhibitory Processing," which he presented at the American Psychiatric Association annual meeting, May 14, 1985.

1. Lawrence C. Kolb. "The Post-Traumatic Stress Disorders of Combat: A Subgroup with a Conditioned Emotional Response," *Military Medicine*, 149 (1984): 237–244.
2. Edward B. Blanchard, Lawrence C. Kolb, Thomas P. Palmeyer and Robert J. Gerardi. "A Psychophysiologic Study of Post-Traumatic Stress Disorder in Vietnam Veterans," *Psychiatric Quarterly*, 54 (1983): 220–228.
3. P. E. Malloy, J. A. Fairbank, and T. M. Keane. "Validation of a Multi-method Assessment of Post-Traumatic Stress Disorder in Vietnam Veterans," *Journal of Consulting and Clinical Psychology*, 51 (1983): 488–494.
4. D. Dobbs and W. P. Wilson. "Observations on Persistence of War Neurosis," *Diseases of the Nervous System*, 21 (1960): 686–691.
5. Sigmund Freud. "Foreword," in Sandor Ferenczi, Karl Abraham, Ernst Simmel, and Ernest Jones, *Psychoanalysis and the War Neurosis*. New York: International Psychoanalytic Press, 1921. See also Freud *Standard Edition*, 17 (1921): 207–210.
6. Sigmund Freud. "Beyond the Pleasure Principle," (1920), in the *Standard Edition*, 18 (1920): 7–64, 26–29.
7. Lawrence C. Kolb. "From Process to Pathology: Chronic Post-Traumatic Stress Disorder of Central Inhibitory Processing," presented at the American Psychiatric Association annual meeting, May 14, 1985.
8. Ibid.
9. N. Q. Brill and G. W. Beebe. *A Follow-up Study of War Neurosis*. V.A. Medical Monograph, Government Printing Office, 1956.

Index